The Outward Bound ®

EARTHBOOK

edited by
LARRY CRENSHAW

> All things are connected.
> —Chief Seattle

> Never doubt that a small group of thoughtful,
> committed citizens can change the world.
> Indeed, it is the only thing that ever has.
> —Margaret Mead

Library of Congress Cataloging-in-Publication Data
EarthBook
    The Outward Bound EarthBook / edited by Larry Crenshaw.
    p.   cm.
    Originally published; EarthBook. 2nd ed. Morganton, N.C. : North
        Carolina Outward Bound School, c1994.
    Includes bibliographical references (p. 224).
    ISBN 0-89732-195-2
    1. Environmental education. 2. Environmental sciences—Study and
    teaching—Activity programs. I. Crenshaw, Larry. II. Title.
GE70.E18 1995
363.7'0071—dc20   95-25199
                                                     CIP

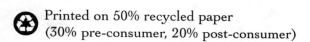 Printed on 50% recycled paper
(30% pre-consumer, 20% post-consumer)

All royalties from the sale of this book will be used for environmental education projects. For permissions, inquiries, ordering information,
or other correspondence, please write:
EarthBook
P.O. Box 43059
Birmingham, AL 35243

Menasha Ridge Press
700 South 28th Street, Suite 206
Birmingham, AL 35233
(800) 247-9437
www.menasharidge.com

North Carolina Outward Bound® School
2582 Riceville Road
Asheville, NC 28805
www.ncobs.org

Table of Contents

Acknowledgements

Thanks to:

• The 130 participants in the 1990 NCOBS All Staff Training who wrote the original activities for this book.

• Steve Teixeira, who organized and coordinated the initial writing.

• CJ Wilson, who took the raw material from All Staff Training and supervised development of the first edition.

• Jeff Menzer and Lawrence Camp, whose energies made the first edition possible.

• Bill Phillips, who made possible the initial publication and dissemination of the EARTHBOOK.

• Jane Snyder and Lelia Ginn, illustrators.

• Other first edition participants, including Cindy Franz, Caroline Blizzard, Buffalo Murray, and Bo Hughes.

• John Huie for his unflagging commitment to environmental education and to the EARTHBOOK.

• Skip Sickler, NCOBS Environmental Coordinator, for logistical help and morale boosting.

• Julia Jitkoff-Partridge, for critical support and guidance.

• Melanie Townsend-Colvin, for level-headed dedicated design work.

• Miriam Newman, for feedback in depth.

• Other advisers and reviewers of materials, including Margo Flood, Nathaniel Frentz, Zachary Frentz, Stephen Guesman, Chris Killion, Lynne Killion, Ellise Mayor, Jeff Menzer, Nikki Sandve, and CJ Wilson.

• Margaret Baxter, whose efforts insured publication of this edition.

• The people at Menasha Ridge Press, who demonstrated that the publishing business can be honorable, informal, and pleasurable.

• Special thanks to Cathy Crenshaw and Arthur Crenshaw for advice, understanding, and support.

Introduction to 3ʳᵈ Edition

Since you're reading this book, you probably already care about the natural world and want to share that caring with others. This is a field guide for learning and teaching about, for thinking and feeling about, and for making connections with the environment.

The EARTHBOOK began as a unique collaboration of 110 staff members of the North Carolina Outward Bound® School on June 5, 1990. The outdoors has always been Outward Bound's classroom. Individual instructors have always taught environmental awareness and appreciation based on their own knowledge and experience. The EARTHBOOK was the first attempt by Outward Bound staff to pool that knowledge, experience, and inspiration into a document that could be useful to themselves and others.

The first edition, coordinated by Steve Teixeira with input from an informal environmental committee, was distributed to Outward Bound schools and staff all over the world.

The second and third editions have expanded the book's audience to include any teacher or parent, any student or friend of the environment, who wants to learn about, teach about, better understand, more fully appreciate, and participate in healing the natural world. It serves as a resource for teachers in public or private schools, leaders in churches or synagogues, instructors in outdoor programs, and groups or families seeking closer connections with the environment.

In the first edition, Steve Teixeira wrote: "We hope every copy of this book gets worn ragged and sees many new additions and editions." The edition you hold is the continuation of a document in process. You are invited to have at it, to wear this book ragged, and to share your ideas, suggestions, quotations, inspirations, and criticisms for its next version.

Internationally, nationally, and at each school, Outward Bound has made commitments to teach awareness of and respect for the natural world. This book reflects and includes many of those commitments, but statements not directly attributed to Outward Bound are the opinions and perspectives of individual EARTHBOOK contributors. An ongoing environmental dialogue among the members of the Outward Bound community will continue as long as Outward Bound exists.

A further note on the activities: Some of these are original creations while others are taken from or influenced by other materials. All known sources of activities have been documented, but with 100+ authors some sources or influences may not be acknowledged.

We have made every effort to get permission for the use of materials. We regret any errors or omissions and look forward to correcting them in future editions.

Larry Crenshaw
Summer, 1995

How to Use This Book

The heart of the book consists of environmental education activities, which are placed in different sections: **Connections, Land, Water, Sky, Fire, The Living World,** and **Global and Local.** In some ways this division is arbitrary, because every subject interconnects with every other. For example. **Land** is formed through and defined by the interplay of **Water, Sky, Fire,** the actions of **The Living World,** and our **Global and Local** activities. the overarching theme of the EARTHBOOK, and of ecology, is **Connections**.

As you use an activity from any section, among your goals should be to see and to show how the activity is connected to other elements of the environment, other subjects of study, and the lives of everyone involved in the activity.

A chart at the beginning of each activity provides basic information for a quick overview. **Time Required,** optimal **Group Size,** and **Materials** needed; the **Location** best suited for the activity and if it is usable or adaptable to the **Indoors;** and what the **Intended Result** of the activity is. This overview should give you a good initial impression about whether or not the activity is appropriate for the group.

Most of the activities are geared toward the outdoors. Obviously, it is easier to get a feel for the environment in the natural world. But every effort has been made to adapt activities or variations to the indoors as well, and most of the EARTHBOOK's activities have indoor components.

Below the chart each activity contains a brief **Summary,** what sort of **Preparation** is required, and the **Procedure.** Some of the activities contain **Background** sections that give you useful environmental information. In most cases there are suggestions for **Follow-up** activities or discussions, and there are **Variations** that add an unusual twist to the activity or give suggestions on how to adapt it for special circumstances.

The activities as written have been tried and tested and should serve instructors well. But feel free to play with and alter the activities–we have tried to create an atmosphere of flexibility that will allow the instructor and participants to adapt activities to their own needs. Outward Bound is committed to experiential education, learning by doing; your activities will be more effective if they involve action. Even if you are satisfied with the activities as written, you should challenge yourself and your students to design additional variations and activities.

Individual activities can be led by a teacher instructor or can be assigned to a member of the group. The group itself can choose someone to lead/facilitate the activity or in some cases may undertake the activity without a leader.

The EARTHBOOK contains not only activities, but quotations and readings. There are readings throughout each section and a collection of readings at the end of each section. Some quotations amplify or reinforce specific activities. Others grapple with the balance people must find between their human-centered and eco-centered needs. Yet others are inspirational statements from some of the great naturalists, ecologists, and nature lovers of the past and present. Groups will enjoy reading these aloud, especially in a natural setting, especially at the end of a day spent outdoors.

All readings are quoted as they were originally written. In many cases this involves the use of male generic pronouns (he, him, his) for both males and females. The editor has chosen to use female generic pronouns (she, her, hers) in the body of the text–these pronouns also refer to both female and male.

For more help on using this book, see "How to Teach About the Environment" in the **Teaching and Learning** section.

CONNECTIONS

John Heine

Connections...

I have learned that nature is not a God or a person or a thing; it is existence and co-existence between the universe and earth and humans and me...
—17 year old Outward Bound student.

I realized that it isn't just "nice" for me to get out into natural beauty—it's essential. It touches a very deep place inside that connects me to the pulse of life.
—37 year old Outward Bound student.

The overarching theme of the EARTHBOOK, and of Ecology, is Connections.

In *The Closing Circle*, biologist Barry Commoner presented Four Laws of Ecology. The First Law: "Everything Is Connected To Everything Else." Chief Seattle and other Native Americans remind us that "All things are connected." The widely-used concept of "the Web of Life" pictures these interconnections as an intricate spiderweb—when strands in that web are broken, all parts of the web suffer. Vietnamese Buddhist monk Thich Nhat Hanh asks us to look at a sunflower and see all that it is—the heat and nourishment of sun, the cool and wet of rain, the many elements of the soil, the air that all living creatures consume and produce, the rest of the stellar universe with which the sun is connected—in short, the sunflower's existence depends upon the existence of everything else. We are all part of Nature's web.

Ecosystems maintain balance through interaction. Predator-prey relationships, the great cycles which turn inorganic into organic into inorganic materials, the cycles which turn sources into wastes into resources: all are part of a complex web of inter-activity. Science, which historically has attempted to understand nature by isolating and studying its parts, has missed many of the great lessons of nature's interconnectedness.

The Second Law of Ecology: "Everything Must Go Somewhere." Over time, ecosystems come into a balance where the waste from one part of a cycle becomes a resource for another part. People are part of ecosystems, but we also have the ability to interfere with and overwhelm them. When human activities impact the cycle of an existing ecosystem, it is impaired and may be damaged or even destroyed. And since ecosystems are connected to one another, stress on one can cause damage to others, sometimes in unforeseeable ways.

The Third Law of Ecology: "Nature Knows Best." Since nature has created its balances over billions of years, the odds are that any human-created system that impacts a natural system is likely to be detrimental to that system. In other words, human R & D (Research and Development) has a long way to go before it can match the depth of Nature's R & D.

The Fourth Law of Ecology: "There Is No Such Thing as a Free Lunch." "Every gain is won at some cost." People cannot, for example, extract fossil fuels and convert them into carbon dioxide, carbon monoxide, and atmospheric particulates without a price being paid somewhere down the line. An ecosystem is thrown out of balance by environmental change. Chances are that life will recover from the stress or collapse of an ecosystem, but the cost may be greater than we would choose to pay—when we threaten and endanger other forms of life, we threaten and endanger ourselves. Which brings us full circle to the First Law of Ecology: Everything Is Connected To Everything Else.

In his essay "The Land Ethic," Aldo Leopold says that land "is a fountain of energy flowing through a circuit of soils, plants and animals." Leopold elaborates three basic ideas:
(1) That land is not merely soil.
(2) That the native plants and animals keep the energy circuit open; others may or may not.
(3) That man-made changes are of a different order than evolutionary changes, and have effects more comprehensive than is intended or foreseen."

Note the similarities between Leopold's basic ideas and Commoner's laws. Leopold then turns to the question of whether or not the land can sustain itself in the face of "man-made changes." He says, "This almost world-wide display of disorganization in the land seems to be similar to disease in an animal, except that it never culminates in complete disorganization or death. The land recovers, but at some **reduced level of complexity**, and with a **reduced carrying capacity** for people, plants, and animals." (Editor's emphasis.)

A friend of Outward Bound writes: "While teaching environmental activities at a camp on Lake Winnipesaukee, I asked people who had lived in the area for most of their lives if they had seen any environmental degradation in the lake. They said no, not really. Within a few hours we saw a crawfish on the edge of the shore and these same people talked about how they rarely saw crawfish any more, how twenty years ago they used to see them, and catch them, every day." The slow decay of environmental systems may make us blind most of the time to the **"reduced level of complexity,"** to the **"reduced carrying capacity."**

Natural systems are stressed—we need to see how we are connected to that stress. Natural systems exist—we need to appreciate them and our connections with them. We need to **explore** out interconnectedness with all other creatures and things.

The activities that follow will help students understand the philosophy expressed by Barry Commoner and Aldo Leopold. They use **observation**, **investigation**, **contemplation**, **appreciation**, and **celebration** to help instructors and students explore **connections**.

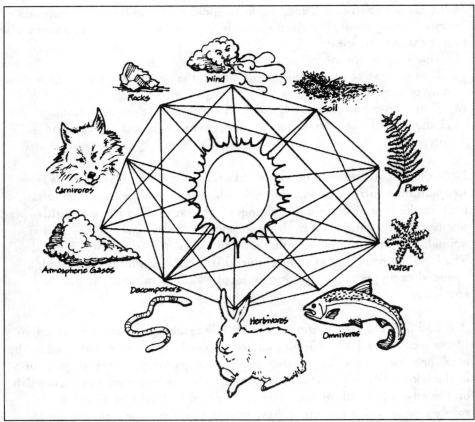

The web of life

I Am Related To You

Time	30 minutes or longer
Group size	Less than 12
Materials	None necessary
Location	Outdoors
Indoor Use	Yes
Intended Result	Fuller appreciation of nature's connections

SUMMARY: Each person makes connections with and between three things, then widens the web of connections to include other things.

PROCEDURE: Have participants take 5-10 minutes to find three objects to which they feel an affinity or attraction. They will not bring the items back, nor even move them, but they will remember where the items are and bring descriptions of them to the group. The items can include human-produced materials, including trash.

When the group is back together, ask each participant to tell why she chose those three things and how they relate to each other. For example, if someone chose a pine cone, a leaf, and a rock: the leaf will decay and become part of the soil to grow the pine tree that produces the pine cone. Parts of the pine cone will decay to become part of the soil to grow the hardwood tree. The pine cone's seeds may take root in the leaf mold and wrap around the rock, so that the rock affects the growth of the tree and the tree continues the process of breaking down the rock. The rock erodes into the soil which gives minerals that helps the trees to grow and produce the leaf and the pine cone.

The rest of the group can help each participant make further connections.

> O leaves, O leaves, I am one with you,
> Of the mould and the sun and the wind and the dew!
> Let the great flood of spring's return
> Float every fear away, and know
> We are all fellows of the fern
> And children of the snow.
> —Bliss Carmen

FOLLOW-UP: Are any of the objects in the circle not related in some way to all of the other objects? Can the group think of anything that can't in some way be related to the larger web of things?

VARIATIONS:
1. Choose an item and pass it around the circle. What emotion does it evoke? If you were an ant, or an elephant, what would this item be or look like to you? (For younger students, this variation can be turned into a game.)
2. Have each student take art materials with her and draw or describe three items without moving them. Have each student take another student or two to the found items and share them in their natural location.
3. Indoors: Have each student draw or write about one or more favorite items, scenes, plants, or animals from the natural world. Use these to illustrate connections.

For most of us, knowledge of our world comes largely through sight, yet we look about with such unseeing eyes that we are partially blind. One way to open your eyes to unnoticed beauty is to ask yourself, "What if I had never seen this before? What if I knew I would never see it again?"
—Rachel Carson

The outstanding scientific discovery of the twentieth century is not television, or radio, but rather the complexity of the land organism. Only those who know the most about it can appreciate how little is known about it. The last word in ignorance is the man who says of an animal or plant: "What good is it?" If the land mechanism as a whole is good, then every part is good, whether we understand it or not. If the biota, in the course of aeons, has build something we like but do not understand, then who but a fool would discard seemingly useless parts? To keep every cog and wheel is the first precaution of intelligent tinkering.
—Aldo Leopold

The Garden Party

Time Required	30 minutes
Group Size	Any
Materials	Paper, tape or pins
Location	Any
Indoor Use	Yes
Intended Result	Better understanding of ecosystem components

SUMMARY: Using ecosystem cards, each student must learn, by seeking hints from other students, which component of the ecosystem she represents.

PREPARATION: Write the name of one component of an ecosystem on each card or piece of paper: birds, fish, water, sunshine, plants, wind, rocks, soil, decomposers, herbivores, omnivores (add more if you have more people). With younger children, use pictures instead of words.

PROCEDURE: Pin or tape a card to each student's back without letting students see their own cards. The group is told that each member represents an integral part of the ecosystem. The students must ask each other yes-no questions to figure out which parts of the ecosystem they represent. Once someone figures out what she is, she can stay involved by helping others guess their identity.

This activity is an excellent lead-in to the Web of Life activity (next page). For the Web, attach the card or paper to the front of each person.

VARIATIONS:
1. Do the Web of Life activity first, since it allows for discussion of terms and reinforces the students' learning.
2. For younger students: do several rounds, letting the students preview cards to be used in that round.

What are you? What am I? Intersecting cycles of water, earth, air and fire, that's what I am, that's what you are.
— John Seed and Joanna Macy

The Web Of Life

Time Required	20 minutes or longer
Group Size	Any
Materials	Ball or string or long rope
Location	Preferably outdoors
Indoor Use	Yes
Intended Result	Understanding of ecosystem interconnectedness

SUMMARY: Members of the group represent parts of the ecosystem and are joined in a web by rope or string to demonstrate interconnectedness.

PREPARATION: Figure out which parts of the ecosystem you will use (or how you will have the students decide which parts they will represent). One possibility is to use "The Garden Party" as an introductory exercise. Part of the ecosystem might include: water, raccoon, hawk, soil, rocks, microorganisms, lichen, deer, etc.

PROCEDURE: After each person is assigned a part, have everyone stand in a circle. Begin uncoiling the rope or string. Each person joins the ecosystem by holding the rope. After the outer circle is made, the remaining rope will be passed within the circle to create a rope web. The person with the rope coil passes it to a part of the ecosystem to which she is directly connected (e.g., plants need sun to live so passes rope to sun; sun affects wind current and passes rope to wind). The person handed the coil stretches the line taut and passes the remaining coil to another part of the ecosystem. Each person describes how she is related to the next component. Every component can be connected many times.

The web will be complete when all parts are connected to one another. If the string runs out first, be sure to emphasize the additional interconnections. Then begin to eliminate components. Have someone drop her lines to simulate extinction. How does this alter the web? How does it affect the rest of the web?

Have individuals stay in place and hold on to their string while someone re-coils, or the string will become tangled. Re-coiling can be a good time to discuss extinction of species and the effects on an ecosystem. Communicate that everything has its purpose—and when one part of the web is interrupted, it affects the whole.

What If?

Time Required	15 minutes or longer
Group Size	Any
Materials	None
Location	Preferably outdoors
Indoor Use	Yes
Intended Result	Increased awareness of environmental issues

SUMMARY: What If questions are asked; answers and ideas lead to other What If questions.

PREPARATION: Choose a topic you want to explore. Think about where the What If questions might lead and prepare for them. Think of questions which will provoke a look at the whole picture as well as questions which look at specific aspects of larger issues. Be prepared to admit your ignorance if the discussion goes beyond your knowledge.

PROCEDURE: A potential What If exercise about the woods through which you are walking might include the following:
  –What if this were an old-growth forest with trees 15 feet around?
  –What would happen when it rains hard in an old-growth forest?
  –What if all the trees were cut down?
  –What would happen when it rains hard on a clearcut?
  –How would the clearcut affect the topsoil? The plant life?
  –What if a road were built to carry the logs out?
  –What if herbicides were used to kill plants beside the road?
  –What if the deer population doubled in this area?
  –What if hunters were allowed to hunt the deer?
  –What if hunters weren't allowed to hunt the deer?
  –What if the loggers logged right up to the edge of the stream?
  –What if the loggers left a 50 foot buffer on either side of the stream?
  –What if the land were twice as steep? What if it were flat?
  –What if this area were planted in Christmas trees?
  –What if it were allowed to regenerate on its own?
  –What if there were a forest fire?
  –What if no more trees were ever cut down?
  –What if no wood products were available for construction?

Use your imagination, and your expertise, to construct What If scenarios. Perhaps your students have areas of expertise as well.

VARIATIONS, Indoors:
1. Assign topics to students that require them to put together What If's. Follow up What If's with study projects or reports.
2. One What If can be pursued in depth. For example, "What if oil prices rise sharply?" Possibilities include: transportation costs go up (people buy more fuel-efficient vehicles, people ride bikes [bike industry booms, people demand bike lanes, etc.], demand rises for electric cars); schools are closed on the coldest days (the school year changes, the travel industry is affected by those changes); Congress opens wildlife refuges to oil exploration (wildlife suffers, environmental interest increases); etc. An extended What If invites in-depth brainstorming and demonstrates how one event, trend, or activity can be connected to many others.

Increasingly, though gradually, we are coming to understand the dimensions, limitations, and uniqueness of our planet. The way ahead is long and difficult with many frustrating cul-de-sacs. Education is an essential component in helping us to map and re-map the way we must go from here.
—James Aldrich and Anne M. Blackburn

We are physically connected, and you can see evidence of this everywhere you look. Think of the fungi that live in the rootstock of trees and plants. The birds that flutter from tree to tree transport fungi spores throughout the environment. Their droppings host a community of insects and microorganisms. When rain falls on the droppings, spores are splashed back up on the tree, creating pockets for life to begin to grow again. This interdependence is an inexorable fact of life; without it, no organism can hope to survive...We are not one living organism, but we constitute a single ecosystem with many differentiated parts. I don't see this as a contradiction, because parts and wholes are nested in each other.
—Lynn Margulis

Scrounge Around

Time Required	30 minutes or longer
Group Size	Any
Materials	Cards
Location	Trail, forest, nature preserve
Indoor Use	No
Intended Result	More knowledge about and appreciation of living things; increased observation skills

SUMMARY: Students search for natural objects and share what they find with one another.

PREPARATION: On cards, write the names of things you want to challenge your students to find—the nature of the items will depend on your expertise and the lessons you want to convey. A botany or zoology class might involve a search for species. Other groups might look for more generic items: an oak tree, a salamander, evidence of mammals, evidence of people, or the group might search for items that call for the use of imagination. For example, cards might contain descriptions such as the following:

Find something that:
—looks like it had a hard winter
—is hopeful
—feels cozy
—makes you smile
—reminds you of your childhood
—agitates you
—reminds you of a good friend
—is heart shaped
—would be a home for an elf
—looks out of place
—came from another planet
—reflects your mood
—feels hard, soft, rough, smooth, slippery
—feels useful, happy, sad, scary, unimportant, important, dead
    (it doesn't have to be alive or dead but feel that way)
—reminds you of a negative quality in yourself
—reminds you of a positive quality in yourself

angry

PROCEDURE: Instruct students not to disturb plants or animals and not to move anything. Each person finds the item, then shares it with others. If up is small the entire group can move together; if large, students can travel in smaller groups or pairs. Once items are pointed out, students trade cards and search again.

A natural community is a tightly grouped assemblage of interdependent members. And what is our role? We are an omnivorous top predator with two lobes of our brain that enable us to imagine what is not present, and two small digital appendages that allow us to make our imaginings concrete. Looking over all the other forms of life on earth, we may represent either an anomaly that will destroy itself or life's ultimate joy in knowing itself. It appears to be up to us.
—Steve van Matre

I will make you brooches and toys for your delight
Of bird-song at morning and star-shine at night.
I will make a palace fit for you and me
Of green days in forests and blue days at sea.

I will make my kitchen and you shall keep your room,
Where white flows the river and bright blows the broom,
And you shall wash your linen and keep your body white
In rainfall at morning and dewfall at night.

And this shall be for music when no one else is near,
The fine song for singing, the rare song to hear!
That only I remember, that only you admire,
Of the broad road that stretches and the roadside fire.
—Robert Louis Stevenson

Readings: Connections

To see a world in a grain of sand
And a heaven in a wild flower;
Hold eternity in the palm of your hand,
And infinity in an hour.
　　　　　　　　—William Blake

In Wildness is the preservation of the world. Every tree sends its fibres
forth in search of the Wild. The cities import it at any price. Men plough
and sail for it. From the forest and wilderness come the tonics and barks
which brace mankind.
　　　　　　　　—Henry David Thoreau

Life consists with wildness. The most alive is the wildest. Not yet subdued
to man, its presence refreshes him...
　　　　　　　　—Henry David Thoreau

I climbed barren mountain-tops. Long tramps led me to desolate valleys
studded with translucent lakes...Solitude, solitude!...Mind and sense develop their sensibility in this contemplative life made up of continual observations and reflections. Does one become a visionary, or, rather, is it not that
one has been blind until then?
　　　　　　　　—Alexandra David-Neel

My credo, abbreviated, goes as follows: There is only one ocean, though its
coves have many names. A single sea of atmosphere with no coves at all.
The miracle of soil, alive and giving life, lying thin on the only planet for
which there is no spare. We need a renewed stirring of love for the Earth.
　　　　　　　　—David Brower

The world's ecosystems are constantly exchanging gases, heat, and nutrients. The Gaia Theory, originated by James Lovelock and supported by scientists and environmentalists worldwide, suggests that the Earth is itself a
giant living organism, and that it is the various life forms themselves that
regulate and maintain conditions necessary to sustain life as we know it.
　　　　　　　　—Will Steger

Despite perceived feelings of superiority over nature, humanity remains fully and totally dependent upon the natural world. We need the bounty of nature to survive on this planet. We need the fresh air to breathe, the clean water to drink, the fertile soil to provide our sustenance.
—Daniel Sitarz

The Earth is one but the world is not. We all depend on one biosphere for sustaining our lives. Yet each community, each country, strives for survival and prosperity with little regard for its impact on others.
—The Brundtland Report

We still talk in terms of conquest. We still haven't become mature enough to think of ourselves as only a tiny part of a vast and incredible universe. Man's attitude toward nature is today critically important simply because we have now acquired a fateful power to alter and destroy nature. But man is a part of nature and his war against nature is inevitably a war against himself...I truly believe that we in this generation must come to terms with nature, and I think we're challenged as mankind has never been challenged before to prove our maturity and our mastery, not of nature, but of ourselves.
—Rachel Carson

We are here to embrace rather than conquer the world.
—Patsy Hallen

Now is the time to share with all life on our maltreated earth by deepening our identification with all life-forms, with the ecosystems, and with Gaia, this fabulous, old planet of ours.
—Arne Naess

It's awkward to talk about a 'relationship with nature,' because the statement itself implies that nature is something different or separate from us. The roots of sustainable culture are in experiences where we are neither opposing nature nor trying to be in communion with it, but rather finding ourselves within it.   —Jonathan White

This is a delicious evening, when the whole body is one sense, and imbibes delight through every pore. I go and come with a strange liberty in Nature, a part of herself.
—Henry David Thoreau

Many times the Indian is embarrassed and baffled by the white man's allusions to nature in such terms as crude, primitive, wild, rude, untamed, and savage. For the Lakota, mountains, lakes, rivers, springs, valleys, and woods were all finished beauty; winds, rain, snow, sunshine, day, night, and change of seasons brought interest; birds, insects, and animals filled the world with knowledge that defied the discernment of man.
—Chief Luther Standing Bear

Hope and the future for me are not in lawns and cultivated fields, not in towns and cities, but in the impervious and quaking swamps.
—Henry David Thoreau

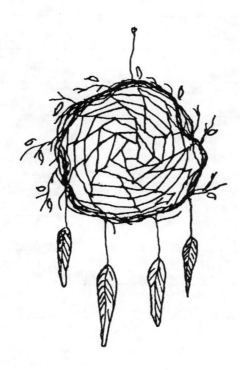

Notes:

LAND

Land...

Everyone in this group said something like, "I wanted to do it because I didn't think I could." It's not like that for me, everything we did I was sure I could do. Positive. It was the earth that gave me strength, it gave me power, it gave me confidence—and energy. Energy that I have been searching for, for so long now. It is here in nature. The sun, trees, ground, rocks, everything is alive here! Everything is giving off such incredible life-energy, you just open your eyes—or take a deep breath. Every breath I take out here feels and tastes so good and cold. So green and young and alive.
— *Outward Bound student, age 18*

The Earth, trees, rocks and sky are exploding with the exuberance of spring, and so am I.
— *Outward Bound student, age 20*

A thin layer of topsoil supports the tremendous variety of life on the land. Organic life and inorganic materials interact—in a small handful of fertile soil there are more living things than there are people on the entire planet. One gram of soil may contain three billion bacteria alone and perhaps an equal number of molds, plus millions upon millions of fungi and algae, plus nematodes, protozoans, and other tiny plants and animals. The land that gives us life is a wonder beyond our comprehending.

The land gives us places to walk, steepnesses to climb, depths to explore. It provides the building blocks for our food, our clothing, our shelter. It gives us beauty in its mountains, its plateaus, its plains, its lowlands, and on its shores, beauty in its landforms, its varieties of strata, its minerals, its gems. Land forms the foundation of our horizons.

We are made of land, of soil, of earth, of mud, of dust. From it we come, to it we return. Here we are. Let us not lose the opportunity we have to touch the earth.

Are You All Right?

Time	15 minutes or longer
Group size	Any
Materials	None
Location	Campsite
Indoor Use	See Variations
Intended Result	Understanding of low impact and no-trace camping; a sense of satisfaction from service

DESCRIPTION: Students search for traces of previous campers, learn about low-impact and no-trace camping, and help improve damaged sites.

PREPARATION: Familiarize yourself with the tenets of low-impact and no-trace camping. See Background Section below.

PROCEDURE: Upon reaching the campsite, before setting up camp, look at the site and consider the impact other humans have had and what impact your own group might have. Negligent campers can traumatize a site—compressing soil, clearing areas of brush, crushing fragile mosses and other plants, damaging trees, disturbing animal habitat, lighting destructive fires, leaving trash and waste. First, study the site for signs of human impact. (Look for signs of impact from animals as well.) Is the soil compacted? Is there erosion? Do you find fire scars, exposed roots, broken tree limbs, stacked rocks? What are the most fragile or easily impacted aspects of this area? Will it handle this group? If the site is too fragile for your group, is there time to move on and find another? If you must use an abused site, how can you minimize your impact?

If no impact is immediately apparent, challenge students to search more carefully. Whether a potential site is overused, well used, or unused, examine it and discuss how your group can have the least impact. If the site has been overused, consider what can be done to heal the piece of land. Let the group determine what they can and are willing to do given time and equipment constraints — how much better are they willing to leave the site than they found it? A campsite service project can be performed while in camp or as you prepare to leave.

Make the minimum goal to erase all signs of your presence as you depart. Go over the site as you did when arriving. Is it better?

VARIATIONS, Classroom:
1. Discuss low-impact camping and abuse of land. Seek camping stories from the class or share your own. Compare low-impact standards with

the high impact activities of a few years ago. Why is there a difference? Emphasize that in all outdoor activities it is important to refrain from willful damage; it is rewarding and challenging to pass through a wilderness, a forest, a park, a field, even a parking lot, and leave it as well off or better than it was found.

2. Find an area of the playground or adjacent land that has been damaged and adopt it. Repair erosion damage, mulch, plant trees, remove trash, build and maintain a path to help protect surrounding land.

There are three ways of trying to win the young. You can preach at them, that is a hook without a worm. You can say, "You must volunteer," that is of the devil. And you can tell them, "You are needed." That appeal hardly ever fails.

—Kurt Hahn (Founder of Outward Bound)

BACKGROUND:

Low-Impact Camping. Camping with respect for the environment is a basic tenet of outdoor education.

National Outdoor Leadership School published *Soft Paths* in 1988 and the pamphlet "Leave No Trace" in 1992. These guides are important collections of low-impact and no-trace ideas and practices. A new edition of *Soft Paths* (Spring, 1995) updates some of the issues and ideas of the first edition. In *Backpacking in the 90's*, Victoria Logue takes low-impact in a different direction: she considers the environmental impact of camping gear and the environmental practices of companies which manufacture the gear. and in *Wilderness Ethics*, the Watermans advocate expanding the definition of low-impact to include behavior in the wild—respecting the land and anyone who might potentially be sharing it.

Note, too, that the philosophy, the science, and the techniques of low-impact and no-trace camping are still being researched. Recommended procedures are changing rapidly. Look for updated editions of the books mentioned above, or call Leave No Trace at (800) 332-4100 for more information.

Obviously, we can't avoid having some impact on the areas we visit. If nothing else, our feet impact the ground over which we walk. But we can minimize our impact and then do enough repair and healing to more than make up for the damage we may have caused.

Outward Bound promotes the standards of the Association for Experiential Education. The environmental standards listed below serve as a basic definition of low-impact and no-trace camping:

—The program does not conduct activities that cause permanent damage to the environment.
—The program conducts activities that leave 'no-traces' on the environment, or when appropriate, only minimal impact on the environment.
—The program respects the wildlife of the area.
—The program respects the local culture, including both social and physical aspects.
—The program selects routes for travel where impact to the environment is minimal. In fragile areas, routes are on trails whenever possible.
—If human waste is disposed in the natural environment, it is done so in a minimally invasive manner. If this cannot be accomplished, it is carried out. If needed, toilet areas are constructed for the type of environment where activities are conducted.
—The program limits the visual impact of its activities.
—Alternatives for soap are pursued first. If any soap is used it is biodegradable and in appropriate portions.
—Washing is conducted at a minimum of 100 feet away from water sources whenever possible.
—Cooking and food handling are conducted in a manner that will not affect or attract animals.
—Food is appropriately stored, and in reusable containers when possible.
—If food is not used, it is carried out. If this cannot be done, it is disposed of in a minimally invasive manner.
—Fires are used only when appropriate.
—Minimal impact techniques for fires are used.
—Tents, tarps, or hammocks are used in place of constructing shelters from surrounding resources.
—Tents, tarps, and hammocks are set up in an environmentally appropriate manner.

—from Manual of Accreditation Standards for
Adventure Programs, 1993, The Association
for Experiential Education. Used with permission.

One Square Foot

Time	30-60 minutes
Group size	Any
Materials	Pencil and paper
Location	Outdoors, the wilder the better
Indoor Use	See Variations
Intended Result	Increased ability "To see the world in a grain of sand;" increased knowledge about the complexity of mini-ecosystems

see p/3 →

SUMMARY: Students are introduced to the idea of one square foot of land as a mini-ecosystem, and different mini-ecosystems are compared and contrasted.

PREPARATION: If you must use a playground or park for this activity, make sure the area you're using has square feet of sufficient complexity—look for a relatively undisturbed area with loose soil and a variety of plants.

PROCEDURE: Prepare students by telling them that even a square foot of land can have a world within it. Inside that square foot area, many things happen daily. Sunshine, rain, dew, wind...animals walk on it or nearby. Bugs, molds, moss live here—and there is an unseen world beyond our magnifying glasses.

Ask participants to write down everything they observe in that square foot (give them a specific amount of time, 5 to 15 minutes).

Some questions to consider:
—What lives there?
—Are there insects? What are they doing?
—What affects the mini-ecosystem?

To the attentive eye, each moment of the year has its own beauty, and in the same field, it beholds, every hour, a picture which was never seen before, and which shall never be seen again.
—Ralph Waldo Emerson

How beautiful a rock is made by leaf shadows!
—John Muir

—What are the sources of food? water? shelter?

—What if you stepped there?

—What if all the trees around were cut down, or what if the field were mowed?

Compare two nearby mini-environments. For example, one may be in full sunlight and one in partial shade, one may be on the north side of a hill or tree and one on the south side, or one may be beside a stream and another away from the stream, or one may be on flat land and one on a steep slope, or one may be all soil and the other mostly rock, or one may be in a field and the other among the roots of a tree.

VARIATIONS:

1. Study the life in a micro-community breaking through asphalt. Compare it with a nearby square foot.
2. Have participants pretend that they are one of the blades of grass or other plants in that square foot and write about their lives.
3. Have them try to see the world with the perspective of one of the small animals in the square foot. What do they see and hear? How does their world feel? Let the participants get down low, face and body to the ground, to help them imagine this one.
4. Have participants go on an insect safari, either following one insect to learn about its life and environment or seeing how many insects, and how many kinds, colors, and sizes of insect, they can find. They should not pick up any of the creatures, however. If the group is likely to handle bugs, discourage them, but also communicate the way to pick up a bug— by its body (not its legs, antennae, or head) and very gently.
5. Have participants write a poem about one of the living things they're observing in their square foot.
6. Gross and Railton (1972) recommend a "One-Hundred-Inch Hike," creeping down a hundred inch path as though it were a jungle, looking for plants other than grass, comparing plants with one another, looking for decaying vegetable and animal matter, feeling soil for moisture.
7. Younger students can wear bug-like antennae (the teacher can set the example), pretend they are insect-evolved life-forms from Mars, and try to learn all they can about their insect relatives in a small (one square foot) sample of Earth's soil.

Earth Time

Time Required	30 minutes
Group Size	Any
Materials	None
Location	Preferably outdoors; quiet place
Indoor Use	Yes
Intended Result	Increased understanding of time beyond human divisions and human scale

SUMMARY: Students use imagination and visualization to learn about time beyond human scale.

Consider the six days of Genesis as a figure of speech for what has in fact been four and a half billion years. On this scale, one day equals something like six hundred and sixty-six million years, and thus, all day Monday and until Tuesday noon, creation was busy getting the world going. Life began Tuesday noon, and the beautiful organic wholeness of it developed over the next four days. At 4 p.m. Saturday the big reptiles came on. Five hours later, when the big redwoods appeared, there were no more big reptiles. Eighteen minutes before midnight the Colorado River started digging the Grand Canyon. Four minutes before midnight something like us — though not really like us — starts to appear. One and a half seconds before midnight we invent agriculture. In the next half second we're so successful that the forests ringing the Mediterranean have disappeared, and with it Sumerian civilization. As it dies, a bristlecone pine sprouts on White Mountain in California, and it's still alive. A third of second before midnight, Buddha is born. A third of a second, Christ. A fortieth of a second before midnight, the Industrial Revolution. An eightieth of a second, we discover oil. We are surrounded with people who think that what we have been doing for the last one-fortieth of a second can go on indefinitely. They are considered normal, but they are stark raving mad.

— David Brower

PROCEDURE: Communicate to your students that we humans in the modern world live by a certain perception of time—measured in seconds, minutes, hours, days, the calendar, and the span of human life. In the natural world, however, the sense of time comes from different cycles. Read aloud the quote from David Brower.

Find a large rock or a large tree with your students, sit down beside it, and invite them to imagine what the world has been like at this place through years and centuries and ages. How did the rocks and trees you see around you get here? What other creatures have lived here? What was it like here millions of years ago?

You might tell your students something like this: Imagine glaciers, oceans and mountains, giant reptiles, bright days and storms, days of struggle and harmony, early humans, more recent natives, modern people. Once the earth was all rock and wind and water. As time went on, life and soil began. Rocks to pebbles to sand to soil to plants to foodstuffs to animals/humans. We are all partly prehistoric rocks, and some of the air we breathe was breathed by dinosaurs. Remind them of the Brower quote—the unfolding of life on the planet was very gradual, very slow.

Use a visualization to help put your students in touch with life here through the ages. A visualization is simply an aid to imagination. There are three important components:

1. Relaxation. Have the participants get comfortable, sitting or lying down. Have them take a few deep breaths, calm themselves, and quiet their minds.

2. Description. Involve the senses as you tell the story ("As continents began to grind into one another, even though that grinding was hundreds of miles from where we sit, the mountains where we are began to rise. The grinding was slow, and the mountains rose very slowly. See the mountains moving upward in small stages, raw stone grumbling, cracking, falling. Feel the earth tremble and hear the roar of rock grating against rock...Now imagine that you live on this same land 6,000 years ago. You live under a rock ledge nearby. Feel a fire warm your skin on a rainy day. Smell the smoke as it lingers under the ledge with you. Your hearing is alert to every change around you—behind the sound of the rain may come the sound of prey or predator. You look about at the lush green of the spring-time forest, breathe in the moist air and the wood smoke, feel the rough rock through your bare feet...").

3. Bring the participants back to the present time as you wrap up the visualization. Aquatic Project Wild offers these suggestions for using guided imagery: "Wait until you see a general state of relaxation before beginning...Remember to speak slowly and steadily. If you want the students

to create rich mental images, you must allow them time to do so. It takes about as much time to observe mental images as it does to carefully review actual physical settings...Once the narrative is finished, invite the students to review all of the images they saw in their minds...After an adequate time for mental review (at least one minute and possibly two minutes), ask the students to open their eyes."

Discuss time cycles for different beings. What does a day mean to a mosquito, which lives for only a few weeks? What does a day mean to a giant redwood, to moss and lichen, to squirrels and owls?

As a group, pretend you can talk to the rock or the tree you are beside; or as individuals, find a tree or rock to spend some time with. Share with it what you hear, see, and smell. Create a mental image and share it with the rock or tree. Talk to it quietly. Imagine it can tell you some of what it has experienced or been part of. Enjoy an imaginative discussion with it. Consider writing the thoughts and images you get from your rock or tree in a poem.

More Thoughts On Time:
As the tempo of modern life has continued to accelerate, we have come to feel increasingly out of touch with the biological rhythms of the planet, unable to experience a close connection with the natural environment. The human time world is no longer joined to the incoming and outgoing tides, the rising and setting sun, and the changing seasons. Instead, humanity has created an artificial time environment punctuated by mechanical contrivances and electronic impulses. Today we have surrounded ourselves with time-saving technological gadgetry, only to be overwhelmed by plans that cannot be carried out, appointments that cannot be honored, schedules that cannot be fulfilled, and deadlines that cannot be met.
—Jeremy Rifkin

My days were not days of the week, bearing the stamp of any heathen deity, nor were they minced into hours and fretted by the ticking of a clock; for I lived like the Puri Indians, of whom it is said that "for yesterday, today, and tomorrow they have only one word, and they express the variety of meaning by pointing backward for yesterday, forward for to-morrow, and overhead for the passing day." This was sheer idleness to my fellow-townsmen, no doubt; but if the birds and flowers had tried me by their standard, I should not have been found wanting.
—Henry David Thoreau

Take time by the forelock. Now or never! You must live in the present, launch yourself on every wave, find your eternity in each moment. Fools stand on their island opportunities and look toward another land. There is no other land; there is no other life but this, or the like of this. Where the good husbandman is, there is the good soil. Take any other course, and life will be a succession of regrets.

— Henry David Thoreau

June 13. Another glorious Sierra day in which one seems to be dissolved and absorbed and sent pulsing onward we know not where. Life seems neither long nor short, and we take no more heed to save time or make haste than do the trees and stars.

— John Muir

It is impossible to meditate on time...without an overwhelming emotion at the limitations of human intelligence.

— Alfred North Whitehead

Topsoil—Gift Of Life

Time Required	10-30 minutes, depending on activity
Group Size	Any
Materials	Shovel or spade, water and water container, knife, and apple
Location	Forest
Indoor Use	Activity 1, 3, 4
Intended Result	An understanding and appreciation of the importance of topsoil

ACTIVITY 1

SUMMARY: A soil cross section is thoroughly examined.

PREPARATION: Knowledge of soil layers.

PROCEDURE: IN THE FIELD—While digging a hole for water or a latrine, try to take out the center as one unit. Examine the layers. Which are from this autumn or last autumn? Previous year? What differences do you see? Name the layers—duff, humus, mineral soil. How was this soil created? What living things help to create soil? (bacteria, fungi, insects, worms, etc.)

PROCEDURE: CLASSROOM—Bring a soil cross-section to class, preferably from a site where the soil was going to be removed. Study it in class.

ACTIVITY 2

SUMMARY: Runoff and erosion in different soil types are demonstrated.

PREPARATION: Study erosion.

PROCEDURE: IN THE FIELD—In an area with a good thick layer of duff and humus, pour a bottle of water from 4-6 feet above the ground. What happens to the water? Find an area without duff or humus and pour the same amount of water from the same height. What happens?

PROCEDURE: CLASSROOM—Pour the water on a slope on school grounds, perhaps a sparsely vegetated area. Compare with thick grass and with a mulched area such as a tree surrounded by pine bark or other cover. Observe the way the water flows, where it pools, what it picks up, how fast it goes under different conditions.

You can also create an erosion project for the classroom. Different types of soils (or soils planted with different densities or types of grass or plants) can be placed (grown) in a slanted tray or box with a notch in the side and drainage holes in the bottom. As water is poured over each surface, varying amounts of soil wash into containers below.

FOLLOW-UP: What physical, mechanical, chemical factors contribute to erosion? What are examples of erosion on a larger scale? What is the largest cause of erosion?

ACTIVITY 3

SUMMARY: An apple is used to demonstrate how much topsoil we have.

PROCEDURE: Hold up the apple. It represents the Earth. Cut away 3/4 of the apple. It represents the percentage of the Earth's surface covered with water.

Hold up 1/4 of the apple. 1/3 of this land can't support life. Cut away 1/3. The remaining apple is 1/6 of the original.

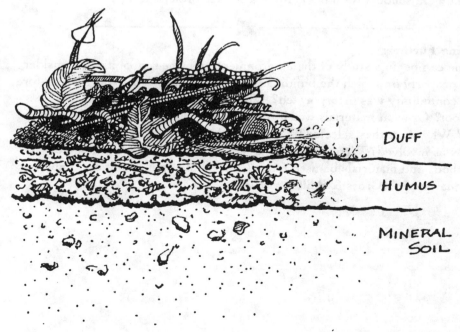

DUFF

HUMUS

MINERAL SOIL

Trim off the peel. Of the 1/6th, this peel represents the precious inches of topsoil we have available on which to live and with which to feed our world population. This topsoil supports virtually all plants and animals that live on land. It filters water, serves as the basis for forests and other land ecosystems, and provides the medium and nutrients which make agriculture possible.

ACTIVITY 4

SUMMARY: Students draw pictures with a topsoil theme.

PROCEDURE: Share the EarthNotes on soil with the group. Brainstorm ways we can protect and replenish the Earth's topsoil. All life depends on these few inches of soil. How can we keep it from washing away? Where does it go when it washes? How does it affect streams and waterways? How does an increasing human population affect topsoil?

Give students the opportunity to draw pictures with a topsoil theme, such as the dependence of humans on topsoil; the dependence of other beings on topsoil; the composition of topsoil; the importance of topsoil. (The local Soil and Conservation Service or some other organization might help sponsor a poster contest.)

What can we do to preserve topsoil on the trail? in our campsites? At home? On school grounds? Is there a service project here?

Going Further:
"One can begin a study of the environment with the school itself. Consider the property on which the building was constructed. What was there before the community was incorporated? Why did this community need this school? Of what materials was it built? What was the source of the materials? Why were they selected? How were they brought here? What processing was involved? What occupations were involved? Would the same methods and materials be used today? This could open a unit on lumbering or quarrying." (Gross & Railton, 1972)

Earth's Natural Resources

Time Required	60-90 minutes
Group Size	Any
Materials	Art supplies
Location	Anywhere
Indoor Use	Yes
Intended Result	Appreciation of our interconnectedness with Earth's resources

SUMMARY: Students use art to learn more about natural resources.

PROCEDURE: Start with discussion (which could take the form of "What If"): What is a "natural resource?" Does the definition of the term assume that these "resources" are there to be exploited by humans? Can anyone think of a better term to describe the wealth, diversity, and intrinsic beauty of the natural world?

What natural materials are available for human use? Which of these "natural resources" are renewable? Which are non-renewable? Which did people live without 200 years ago? 1000 years ago? How would our society change if we ran out of fossil fuels?

Have students identify natural resources which were the source for clothing, food, shelter, etc. (e.g., look at your shoes or shorts—what are they ultimately made of? Trace them all the way back to the Earth. See *What's the Connection*, page 132).

Have the group make a collage or other collaborative artwork depicting natural resources in any way, concrete or abstract, that they wish. They can choose to focus on one resource or show many different ones. They can work as a group, or in smaller groups, or as individuals.

Ideas for topics/themes include geology, plants, cycles (water, soil, air, reproduction), and tracing an item from Earth to its current use. Finished pieces can be mailed to someone—the school director, a friend, parents, the President, Secretary of the Interior, etc.

Beauty beyond thought everywhere, beneath, above, made and being made forever. I gazed and gazed and longed and admired.
—John Muir

Tuning In To Earth's Voices

Time Required	30 minutes
Group Size	Any
Materials	None
Location	Quiet outdoors
Indoor Use	No
Intended Result	Enhanced sensitivity toward the natural world

SUMMARY: Students contemplate and make quiet attempts to connect with the natural world.

PROCEDURE: It helps to do this activity when the group is ready and willing to be quiet and meditative.

Ask students to let go of other thoughts and be aware of the sights, smells, and sounds around them.

A participant names something nearby—a tree, rock, or insect; the land, the sky, the brook; the forest, the community of life, the ecosystem. Ask the group to be quiet for several minutes, and then ask, "What does it say?" The members of the group each tell what the named item says to them before the namer says what she hears. Whether it is interpreted to be "Earth's voice" or the group's impressions of the Earth and their relationship with it, the result of this exercise can be sensitive appreciation of and concern for the natural world.

VARIATIONS:
1. Break into small groups if numbers are too large or if you think smaller groups will work better together.
2. Consider having a group member serve as scribe and write down what everyone says.
3. Let the impressions be written rather than spoken, or let everyone write down impressions first, then have the option of communicating them if the atmosphere is right.
4. Have a scribe write down words and phrases as people speak; then have the group create a poem using them.
5. Lead a silent walk and point out things as you go. Have the person behind you point out the thing to the person following. Go slowly, leaving time (20-30 seconds) for individuals to write down words or phrases that come to mind as they look at each thing. Afterwards, go around 2-3 times taking words or phrases from each person's notes, putting them together to create a poem.

In "Wood Notes," Ralph Waldo Emerson has a pine tree speaking. It says, in part:

Behind thee leave thy merchandise,
Thy churches and thy charities,
And leave thy peacock wit behind;
Enough for thee the primal mind
That flows in streams, that breathes in wind;
Leave all thy pedant lore apart;
God hid the whole world in thy heart,
Love shuns the sage, the child it crowns,
Gives all to them who all renounce.
The rain comes when the wind calls,
The river knows the way to the sea,
Without a pilot it runs and falls,
Blessing all lands with its charity.
The sea tosses and foams to find
Its way up to the cloud and wind...
And thou—go burn thy wormy pages,
Shalt outsee the seer, and outwit sages.

Ridge Aerobics

Time Required	10 minutes or longer
Group Size	Any
Materials	Topographical maps
Location	Any
Indoor Use	Yes
Intended Result	More knowledge of maps

SUMMARY: Students learn about map reading using a variation of Simon Says.

PREPARATION: Understanding of relief maps.

PROCEDURE: Play Ridge Aerobics like Simon Says, with instructors calling out words and the group showing the appropriate formations with their arm and body movements.

First, teach the arm positions for each geographic feature:

Valley: Arms up on two sides, bend upper body 90 degrees to the left, one arm up, one arm down.

Ridge: Arms down on two sides, bend upper body 90 degrees to the right, one arm up, one arm down.

Mountain peak: Turn in a circle with both arms down.

Saddle or Gap: Arms up on two sides, rotate 90 degrees, arms down on two sides, rotate back.

Teach participants to identify formations on a topographical map. Repeat ridge aerobics showing the formations instead of calling out their names.

Make up your own for: Plateau, Crater, Flatland, Canyon, etc. Or create variations that use the whole body.

VARIATIONS:

1. Create three dimensional models of landscapes using sand or Playdoh.
2. Explain contour lines by drawing them around your knuckles.
3. Classroom: Use slides or projections of maps to show features and have students respond to each picture with the proper position.

EarthNotes: Land

The planet Earth weighs 6,586,000,000,000,000,000,000,000 tons. Its surface is 196,940,000 square miles. 57,506,000 square miles, or 29.2%, is dry land. 139,434,000 square miles, or 70.8%, is water on top of (wet) land. (Cousteau, 1981)

The planet travels a distance of 580,000,000 miles in its orbit around the sun, traveling at a speed of 66,705 miles per hour. Its rotational velocity at the equator is 1,037 miles per hour. (Cousteau, 1981)

"Eleven percent of the world's land is used to grow crops; perhaps 2 per cent is paved over or covered by cities and towns; a quarter serves as pasture for livestock; and most of the 30 percent that is still forested is exploited at some level by humanity or has been converted to tree farms. Nearly all the remaining third of Earth's land is in arctic or antarctic regions or desert, or it's too mountainous or otherwise too inhospitable to be of much use to civilization." (Ehrlich & Ehrlich, 1990)

"Almost 5 percent of the world's landmass is now either totally or partially protected as parks and reserves, not including Antarctica." (World Resources Institute, 1992)

"Global soil losses in excess of new soil formation have been estimated at 24 to 26 billion tons per year." (Ehrlich & Ehrlich, 1990)

"Erosion makes soil less able to retain water, depletes it of nutrients, and reduces the depth available for roots to take hold. Land productivity declines. Eroded topsoil is carried to rivers, lakes, and reservoirs; silts up ports and waterways; reduces reservoir storage capacity; and increases the incidence and severity of floods." (The Brundtland Report, 1987)

"Over the past 45 years, about 11 percent of the Earth's vegetated soils became degraded to the point that their original biotic functions are damaged, and reclamation may be costly or in some cases impossible." (World Resources Institute, 1992)

"Amount of prime farmland in the United States—344 million acres. 48 million acres have been lost since 1967, mostly from conversion to urban or built-up areas or water impoundments. "The loss of prime farmland puts more pressure on use of less suitable farmland that generally is more susceptible to erosion or drought, more difficult to cultivate, and usually less productive." (Council on Environmental Quality, Executive Office of the President, 1992)

"Around 1980, the United States was estimated to be losing nearly 4 billion tons of soil a year, enough to fill a freight train 600,000 miles long — 24 times the circumference of Earth. About a third of America's cropland is affected, and drops in yield attributable to erosion have already been noted, including a 2 percent decline in grain production per acre in Illinois — in the richest part of the grain belt — between 1979 and 1984." (Ehrlich & Ehrlich, 1990)

"Recently, though, the U.S. Department of Agriculture's new Conservation Reserve Program slashed the national erosion rate by a third in just a couple of years — one of the biggest conservation success stories of the century." (Ehrlich & Ehrlich, 1990)

"Without conservation measures, the total area of rain fed cropland in developing countries in Asia, Africa, and Latin America will shrink by 544 million hectares over the long term because of soil erosion and degradation..." (The Brundtland Report, 1987)

Farm Fertilizer Use in the United States	1940 — 1.8 million tons
	1950 — 4.1 million tons
	1960 — 7.5 million tons
	1970 — 16.1 million tons
	1980 — 23.1 million tons
	1990 — 20.6 million tons
Farm Pesticide Use in the United States	1964 — 291 million pounds
	1971 — 464 million pounds
	1982 — 552 million pounds
	1991 — 478 million pounds

(Source: The Council on Environmental Quality, 1992)

Readings: Land

Now I see the secret of the making of the best persons,
It is to grow in the open air, and to eat and sleep with the earth.
—Walt Whitman

I learned to walk with the wilderness rather than waltzing with society.
—*15 year old Outward Bound student*

Shall I not have intelligence with the earth? Am I not partly leaves and vegetable mould myself?
—Henry David Thoreau

Whoso walketh in solitude,
And inhabiteth the wood...
On him the light of star and moon
Shall fall with purer radiance down;
All constellations of the sky
Shed their virtue through his eye.
Him Nature giveth for defence
His formidable innocence,
The mounting sap, the shells, the sea,
All spheres, all stones, his helpers be.
—Ralph Waldo Emerson

Perhaps we cannot statistically prove that people who are more connected to the earth are wiser and healthier and happier, but common sense tells us that it must be so.
—Steve van Matre

Come, heart, where hill is heaped upon hill:
For there the mystical brotherhood
Of sun and moon and hollow and wood
And river and stream work out their will;
And God stands winding His lonely horn,
And time and the world are ever in flight;
And love is less kind than the grey twilight,
And hope is less clear than the dew of the morn.
—William Butler Yeats

The forest about us was dense and cool, the sky above us was cloudless and brilliant with sunshine, the broad lake before us was glassy and clear, or rippled and breezy, or black and storm-tossed, according to Nature's mood; and its circling border of mountain domes, clothed with forests, scarred with landslides, coven by canyons and valleys, and helmeted with glittering snow, fitly framed and finished the noble picture. The view was always fascinating, bewitching, and entrancing. The eye was never tired of gazing, night or day, in calm or storm; it suffered but one grief, and that was that it could not look always, but must close sometimes in sleep.
— Mark Twain

All ethics so far evolved rest upon a single premise: that the individual is a member of a community of interdependent parts. His instincts prompt him to compete for his place in the community, but his ethics prompt him also to co-operate...The land ethic simply enlarges the boundaries of the community to include soils, waters, plants, and animals, or collectively: the land...In short, a land ethic changes the role of Homo sapiens from conqueror of the land-community to plain member and citizen of it. It implies respect for his fellow-members, and also respect for the community as such.
— Aldo Leopold

Crossing a bare common, in snow puddles, at twilight, under a clouded sky, without having in my thoughts any occurrence of special good fortune, I have enjoyed a perfect exhilaration. I am glad to the brink of fear.
— Ralph Waldo Emerson

When I left college I moved to the country and started gardening for the first time. I could spend hours with the soil on my hands — it felt like I was drawing strength from the Earth. At age 22 I had the feeling that my education was finally beginning. Then I moved to the city and lost the connection. Years later, on my Outward Bound course, I was in touch with the Earth again. I kept trying to understand my elation and the intensity of my feelings and the sense of intellectual expansiveness I felt. The day before the course ended I was finally able to put it into words: "The love of the land is the beginning of learning."
— *Outward Bound student, age 38.*

WATER

Water...

While I'm on my solo, laying by the stream, I wonder why I cannot go to sleep and have a beautiful dream; Then I hear a voice, not a person, it's coming from the stream; Am I going crazy, I cannot have a dream; Because the stream I'm laying beside is talking to me.

—15 year old Outward Bound student

Earth is the blue planet. Virtually all the water that has existed and will exist is on the Earth right now. This "life fluid" flows in a continuous cycle through plants and animals, ground and sky. The very water that irrigates rice fields in Malaysia may have been contained in the cup of poisonous hemlock tea that Socrates drank. Water that will provide nutrients for kelp beds in California may be part of the tear in your eye.

Why is water so important to us? We need it to survive—and we use it every day. Each of us is 75% water. We drink it, we bathe in it, we canoe over and through it. And yet this resource that is so essential to us is in danger of irreparable damage. Factories pollute the sky; oil, plastics, and garbage pollute the ocean; toxic wastes and poorly planned sanitation systems pollute the groundwater, rivers, and lakes.

What can we do? We can start by becoming more aware and learning about the problems and solutions. We can act, making choices that conserve water in our homes, businesses, and schools; advocating and working for policies and laws that keep water clean; educating others about the wonder and fragility of this treasure.

The next time it rains, remember it is all part of the cycle. Rain helps the plants grow, gives us drinking water, gives us bigger rapids in the river. Don't take cover. Go out and walk in it. Dance, jump, and sing in the rain.

THE WATER CYCLE

All water on our planet is connected, and all goes through the stages of the water cycle (or hydrological cycle). Ocean water evaporates, forms clouds, condenses into rain. When it reaches the ground, a raindrop may join other water on the surface, flowing back through streams and rivers to the sea. Or it may take a detour through a plant, being soaked up by the roots and released into the air through the leaves. An animal or a human may join part of its cycle. Or it may soak through the soil and join groundwater. Water may become part of a glacier or icecap, or spend many thousands of years at the bottom of the sea. But virtually all the water we have ever had and will ever have is present on the planet now.

A water molecule spends an average of 9 days in the atmosphere. When it reaches a river its average time on its journey to the sea is 2 weeks. If it joins the soil it could stay there for between 2 weeks and a year. A water molecule might stay 10 years in a large lake, 100 years in shallow ground-water, 120 years in shallow ocean water. Or it might spend 3,000 years in deeper ocean, 10,000 years in deep groundwater, or 10,000 years in the Antarctic icecap. (Cousteau, 1981)

As it travels through its cycle, water is filtered and cleaned of pollutants and contaminants. When we overpollute water, when we pollute it at a rate faster than it can be cleaned, we harm the life that needs it for survival. We harm the phytoplankton (plant plankton) in the ocean, which produces at least 1/3 of the oxygen for the planet. We harm the small animals and plants that live in or near the water and the larger animals that depend on them. We harm ourselves.

A Toast To Water

Time Required	15 minutes
Group Size	Any
Materials	Water, cups
Location	Any
Indoor Use	Yes
Intended Result	Fuller understanding of the water cycle, better appreciation of water

SUMMARY: Students learn about the water cycle by drinking toasts to its elements.

PROCEDURE: Talk about the water cycle and the fact that water is recycled again and again. Ask your students to think of all the places that have water, such as icecaps and glaciers, groundwater and surface water, streams and rivers, plants and animals, clouds and sewers.

Make sure each student has a cup. Pour water into each cup as if the liquid were a fine wine or a magic elixir. You might talk about the immediate source of this water, where it came from and how it has been treated for human consumption. Then take the water backwards step by step, showing that this water participated in many parts of the water cycle and has probably participated in all parts. Ask them to think and imagine where the water they are about to drink could have been—at any time in history or anywhere on earth. The group raises its glasses and echoes each toast, then takes a small sip of water. For example:

"This water was once part of a dinosaur. To the dinosaurs."
　　Everyone responds, "To the dinosaurs," and all drink.
"This water was once part of a city's sewage." "To sewage."
"This water was once drunk by an Egyptian who is now a mummy in the British Museum." "To the Egyptians."
"This water was once part of a glacier a mile high over what is now the Great Lakes." "To the glacier."
"This water was once in an earthworm." "To the earthworm."

FOLLOW-UP:

1. Think about where this water will go in the future, talk about its immediate pathways from where you are, and drink a few toasts to places where it might end up. "This water will someday go down the Mississippi River from Minnesota to the sea." "To the Mississippi." "This water will live in the deepest part of the ocean for 10,000 years." "To the deepest part of the ocean."

2. The students should be reminded that drinking water can be just as satisfying as drinking cola. It's also much healthier.

Adapted from Groundwater: Illinois' Buried Treasure (Environmental Education Association of Illinois, 1993). Used with permission.

HOW MUCH WATER IS THERE?

Approximately	326,000,000 cubic miles
Of this the ocean has	317,000,000 cubic miles
Leaving	9,000,000 cubic miles
Of this, icecaps and glaciers have	7,000,000 cubic miles
Leaving	2,000,000 cubic miles
Of this, subsurface groundwater is	2,000,000 cubic miles
Leaving	0????

Since the above numbers were rounded, the numbers that follow are almost infinitesimally insignificant. Yet on them our lives depend:

Fresh water lakes have	30,000 cubic miles
Saline lakes and inland seas have	25,000 cubic miles
Soil moisture has	16,000 cubic miles
The atmosphere has	3,100 cubic miles
And rivers and streams have only	300 cubic miles

(Source: Leopold et al., Water, 1966.)

One mathematician has calculated that if Columbus spilled a glass of drinking water into the sea back in 1492—and if that glass of water was by now thoroughly mixed in all the oceans and rivers of the world, then "every glass of water drawn from every faucet in the world would contain as many as 250 molecules from the original water Columbus had spilled from his glass." Just a single drop of water has 1,700,000,000,000,000,000 (1.7 quintillion) molecules.
—Robert Hendrickson

Earth's Water To Go

Time Required	15 minutes
Group size	Any
Materials	5 gallon container, measuring cup, spoon, journal and pens
Location	Any
Indoor Use	Yes
Intended Result	An understanding of the relative quantities of water on the planet

SUMMARY: With a 5 gallon container as a prop, students learn about how much water the planet has and how it's distributed.

PROCEDURE: Fill a 5 gallon container with water. On the trail this can be a pack liner. The 5 gallons represents all of the water on the planet. (See previous page for actual volumes this represents.)

Take out two cups. This represents all of the fresh water in the world—the rest is in the oceans.

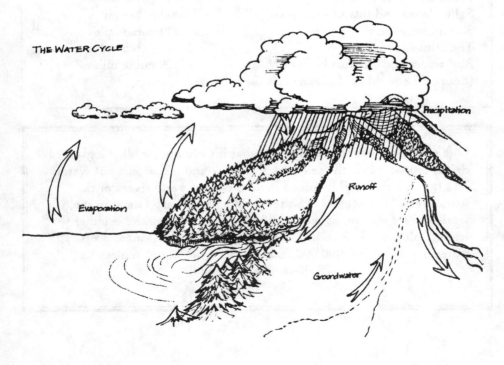

THE WATER CYCLE

Precipitation

Runoff

Evaporation

Groundwater

Remove one and one-half of those two cups. This is freshwater in ice-caps and glaciers.

Of the remaining half cup, take out 1/4 teaspoon. This represents all freshwater lakes. The rest is deep ground water. Of the 1/4 teaspoon, take out 1/2 drop. This represents all freshwater streams and rivers.

End the activity with one small drop of water on your finger. Ask participants to write a story about this drop, and where it might have been over the millennia. Have them pretend that they are the drop and write about their lives.

FOLLOW-UP: All the water we have on Earth right now is all we will ever have. It is a limited quantity. It is theoretically possible to obtain all the freshwater we need, from the oceans for example, but the high energy use involved will not allow unfettered use of water. We need to learn to live with water as a renewable resource, using as little as possible, conserving as much as we can, returning used water to the ecosystem in as clean a state as we received it.

VARIATION: Mathematically minded students can figure out the relative amounts of water another way. Five gallons of water is 1280 tablespoons. How many tablespoons represent all the sea water in the world? How many all the icecaps and glaciers? Etc. The amount represented by rivers is less than 1/1000th of a tablespoon.

Sources for this exercise include *Aquatic Project Wild* and *Groundwater: Illinois' Buried Treasure.*

Waterfall Game

Time Required	45 minutes or longer
Group size	8-15
Materials	Background information
Location	Along a stream or other aquatic environment
Indoor Use	No
Intended Result	Increased knowledge of water issues; increased ability and enjoyment through peer teaching

DESCRIPTION: Students teach one another about water in an outdoor environment.

PREPARATION: Background information is needed on the topics to be taught by the students. Students choose or are assigned a topic. The location where each student will have her station is chosen. Stations should be at or near water and close to one another.

EXAMPLES OF WATERFALL STATIONS: Water cycle • Plant uses and activity at water source • Riverbed composition (sand, mud, rock) • Human water needs • Stream flow patterns (eddies, waves) and their causes • Animal use of water (drinking and habitat) • Water pollution • Water and transportation • Water and spirituality • Water and power • Droughts • Floods • Fishing • Sunlight on Water • Water and recreation • (Add Your Own)

Every rain-cloud, however fleeting, leaves its mark, not only on trees and flowers whose pulses are quickened, and on the replenished streams and lakes, but also on the rocks are its marks engraved whether we can see them or not.
— John Muir

PROCEDURE: Each student now has a topic which she has chosen or been assigned, and each student has a station at which she will teach. The stations are close to one another on a trail. Assuming there are nine participants:

Each student spends a few minutes at her individual station reviewing her topic and thinking about how she will want to present it to the other students. After a few minutes of preparation, students return to a central meeting area. Student #1 goes to Station #1, and then every two minutes a new student goes out. Student #2 goes to Station #1 and is taught by Student #1, then goes on to Station # 2. Student # 3 is taught by Student #1, then moves on to Student # 2, then moves to Station # 3. After Student # 9 leaves Station # 1, Student # 1 waits two minutes then moves to Station #2, and so on. Each student will teach and be taught one on one by every student.

"Nice? It's the only thing," said the Water Rat solemnly, as he leant forward for his stroke. "Believe me, my young friend, there is nothing—absolutely nothing—half so much worth doing as simply messing about in boats. Simply messing," he went on dreamily: "messing—about—in—boats...Nothing seems really to matter, that's the charm of it. Whether you get away, or whether you don't; whether you arrive at your destination or whether you reach somewhere else, or whether you never get anywhere at all, you're always busy, and you never do anything in particular; and when you've done it there's always something else to do, and you can do it if you like, but you'd much better not. Look here! If you've really nothing else on hand this morning, supposing we drop down the river together and have a long day of it?"

—Kenneth Grahame

Creek Observation

Time Required	1 hour or longer
Group size	8-15
Materials	Pen and paper
Location	Small creek
Indoor Use	No
Intended Result	Increased awareness and insight through solitude and attunement

SUMMARY: Students spend quiet time to observe the world along a creek.

PROCEDURE: Each student chooses or is assigned a small section, a few linear feet, of a creek and observes that section. Students can take notes of what is happening there, what lives in the air, what enters and leaves, what they hear while they are sitting there, their thoughts and feelings.

Students can bring observations, thoughts, and feelings back to the group. They can also introduce others to their areas.

Journal ideas:

Write a page about your section of creek.

What would it be like to live here?

How would it change as the seasons change?

What was it like 100 years ago? 1000?

What signs do you see of aquatic insects? the decay process? water purification process? Mammals? What other creatures do you think come to this stream?

> O glide, fair stream! Forever so,
> Thy quiet soul on all bestowing,
> Till all our minds forever flow
> As thy deep waters now are flowing.
> —William Wordsworth

Explore An Ecosystem

Time Required	45 minutes or longer
Group size	Any
Materials	Paper and pen
Location	A wild ecosystem
Indoor Use	No
Intended Result	More knowledge about the components of a particular ecosystem

SUMMARY: Students put together components and processes of an ecosystem by moving through it quietly and observantly.

PREPARATION: Learn appropriate background information about the ecosystem you will be exploring. Find out about the area by talking with a ranger, a biologist, or another appropriate expert: What species are likely to be present? What processes (camouflage, predator/prey, interdependence, etc.) are present? What interesting stories can be told about the area, its flora, its fauna? While the example below is aquatic, the exercise is also appropriate for land ecosystems.

PROCEDURE:
1. Discuss briefly the components of your ecosystem. The following example might be used in the red mangrove ecosystem, which is in the Florida Everglades:
   - green leaves
   - detritus
   - snook
   - lobster
   - birds
   - decaying leaves
   - crab
   - red fish
   - jellyfish
   - high tide line
   - yellow leaves
   - minnow
   - larval shrimp
   - snail
2. Discuss the processes that are at work in the ecosystem, such as:
   - decay
   - predator/prey
   - succession
   - adaptation
   - interdependence
   - camouflage
   - food cycle
   - diversity
   - fertilization
3. Enter the ecosystem and challenge students to find as many of the items or signs of the processes as possible. Allow 10-15 minutes.
4. Use cards/cardboard or newsprint and have individuals draw their representation of the food chain, food cycle, adaptation, or another process.
5. Incorporate a 15 minute or longer silent sit.

VARIATION: Use what you've learned from the study of an ecosystem for the *Web of Life* (page 8).

Stream Quality Survey

Time Required	45 minutes or longer
Group size	8-15
Materials	Background information, sieve or screen, garbage bag, water sprayer
Location	Along a stream or other aquatic enviroment
Indoor Use	No
Intended Result	Increased awareness of water quality issues; enhanced ability to work as part of a team

DESCRIPTION: Students participate in a stream quality survey by searching for and identifying insect species which indicate stream quality.

PREPARATION: Familiarize yourself with the insects and other animals illustrated below. Be aware of the ones you will be most likely to find in your area.

PROCEDURE: The following activity is part of and an adaptation of a full stream quality survey from Save Our Streams, a program of the Izaak Walton League of America. It is used with permission. It is for exploring stream quality at a site with a rocky bottom. The Izaak Walton League also has a survey method for muddy bottom sampling.
1. Selecting a site: Select a riffle typical of the stream, that is, a shallow fast-moving area with a depth of 3-12 inches and cobble-sized stones (2-10 inches) or larger.
2. Positioning the net: Place your kick seine or screen at the downstream edge of the riffle. Be sure that the bottom of the seine or screen fits tightly against the stream bed. You may want to use rocks to hold the net down tightly. You want to be sure no insects can escape over the top of or underneath the net.
3. Collecting the sample: Monitor the stream bed for distance of 3 feet upstream of the screen. Firmly and thoroughly rub your hands over all rock surfaces (top, sides, and bottom) to dislodge any attached insects. Carefully place any large rocks outside of your 3 foot sampling area after you have rubbed off any macroinvertebrates. Stir up the bed with hands and feet until the entire 3 foot square area has been worked over. All detached insects will be carried into the net. For 60 seconds, and no longer, kick the stream bed with a sideways motion towards the net. Disturb the first few inches of sediment to dislodge burrowing organisms.
4. Removing the net: When Step 3 is completed, remove the screen with a

forwards scooping motion. The idea is to remove the net without allowing any insects to be washed from its surface.

5. Picking your sample: Place the net on a flat, well-lit area. Examine the different types of insects you see. Look closely, since most insects are only a fraction of an inch long. You may want to place a white trash bag under the net before picking the sample in order to catch any tiny critters that crawl through the net. You might also want to use a watering can to periodically water your net. Critters will stop moving as the net dries. Occasionally wetting the net will cause the critters to move, making them easier to spot. (It also helps to keep them alive.) Watering the net is especially important on hot, dry days.

WATER QUALITY INDICATORS:	
In the case of	Look for
Little variety of insects with great abundance of each kind	Water overly enriched with organic matter
Only one or two kinds of insects in great abundance	Severe organic pollution
A variety of insects, but only a few of each kind, or no insects, but the stream appears clean	Toxic pollution

STREAM PROBLEMS AND THEIR IMPACTS ON STREAM ORGANISMS:

1. PHYSICAL PROBLEMS: May include excessive sediment from erosion, street runoff, or a discharge pipe. Sediment may create poor riffle characteristics, contribute to excessive flooding, reduce flow, change temperature, and smother aquatic life. The result is usually a reduction in the number of all animals in the study area.

2. ORGANIC POLLUTION: Is from excessive human or livestock wastes or high algae populations. The result is usually a reduction in the number of different kinds of insects, leaving more collectors/scrapers.

3. TOXICITY: Includes chemical pollutants such as chlorine, acids, metals, pesticides, and oil. The result is usually a reduction in the number of insects.

A survey such as this stresses the ecosystem you are exploring. Attempt to return the area you survey to the way it was when you found it.

FOLLOW-UP: How are streams polluted? How much pollution comes from human activity? How much from non-human factors?

Going Further:
1. Consider participating in a fuller stream survey, returning to this site every two months to do the more extensive stream quality survey. In the United States, federal, state, and local governments monitor around 30% of the nation's rivers and streams. Volunteer monitoring data helps fill the gaps. Results can be sent to the Izaak Walton League. For further information on water issues, how to conduct a full stream survey, or where to obtain equipment and expertise for more comprehensive water testing, write: Save Our Streams Program; Izaak Walton League of America; 1401 Wilson Blvd., Level B; Arlington, VA 22209. (703) 528-1818
2. Become a stream scout. The Izaak Walton League also has information on telling the difference between sick and healthy streams. They advise trying to find the source of pollution and alerting government officials. You might also enlist the help of an environmental group or local media if industries are violating water laws.

Stream Insects and Crustaceans

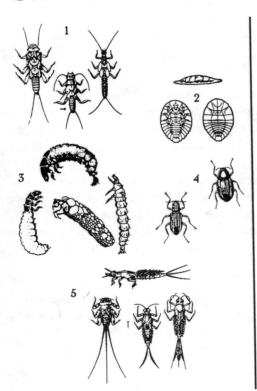

GROUP ONE TAXA
Pollution sensitive organisms found in good quality water.

1. *Stonefly: Order Plecoptera.* 1/2" - 1 1/2", 6 legs with hooked tips, antennae, 2 hair-like tails. Smooth (no gills) on lower half of body. (See arrow.)

2. *Caddisfly: Order Trichoptera.* Up to 1", 6 hooked legs on upper third of body, 2 hooks at back end. May be in a stick, rock, or leaf case with its head sticking out. May have fluffy gill tufts on lower half.

3. *Water Penny: Order Coleoptera.* 1/4", flat saucer-shaped body with a raised bump on one side and 6 tiny legs on the other side. Immature beetle.

4. *Riffle Beetle: Order Coleoptera.* 1/4", oval body covered with tiny hairs, 6 legs, antennae. Walks slowly underwater. Does not swim on surface.

5. *Mayfly: Order Ephemeroptera.* 1/4" - 1", brown, moving, plate-like or feathery gills on sides of lower body (see arrow), 6 large hooked legs, antennae, 2 or 3 long, hair-like tails. Tails may be webbed together.

6. *Gilled Snail: Class Gastropoda.* Shell opening covered by thin plate called operculum. Shell usually opens on right.

7. *Dobsonfly (Hellgrammite): Family Corydalidae.* 3/4" - 4", dark-colored, 6 legs, large pinching jaws, eight pairs feelers on lower half of body with paired cotton-like gill tufts along underside, short antennae, 2 tails and 2 pairs of hooks at back end.

GROUP TWO TAXA

Somewhat pollution tolerant organisms can be in good or fair quality water.

8. *Crayfish: Order Decapoda.* Up to 6", 2 large claws, 8 legs, resembles small lobster.

9. *Sowbug: Order Isopoda.* 1/4" - 3/4", gray oblong body wider than it is high, more than 6 legs, long antennae.

10. *Scud: Order Amphipoda.* 1/4", white to grey, body higher than it is wide, swims sideways, more than 6 legs, resembles small shrimp.

11. *Alderfly larva: Family Sialidae.* 1" long. Looks like small hellgrammite but has 1 long, thin, branched trail at back end (no hooks). No gill tufts underneath.

12. *Fishfly larva: Family Corydalidae.* Up to 1 1/2" long. Looks like small hellgrammite but often a lighter reddish-tan color, or with yellowish streaks. No gill tufts underneath.

13. *Damselfly: Suborder Zygoptera.* 1/2" - 1", large eyes, 6 thin hooked legs, 3 broad oar-shaped tails, positioned like a tripod. Smooth (no gills) on sides of lower half of body. (See arrow.)

14. *Watersnipe Fly Larva: Family Athericidae (Atherix).* 1/4" -1", pale to green, tapered body, many caterpillar-like legs, conical head, feathery "horns" at back end.

15. *Crane Fly: Suborder Nematocera.* 1/3" - 2", milky, green, or light brown, plump caterpillar-like segmented body, 4 finger-like lobes at back end.

16. *Beetle Larva: Order Coleoptera.* 1/4" - 1", light-colored, 6 legs on upper half of body, feelers, antennae.

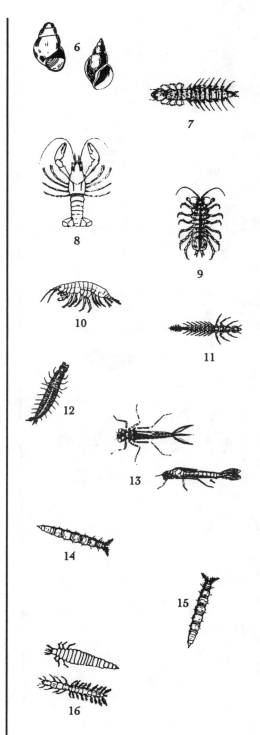

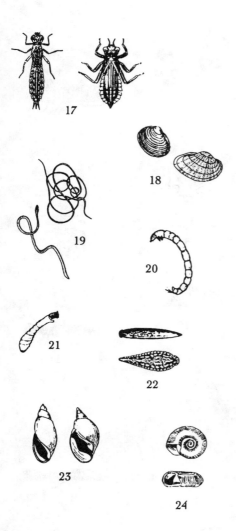

17. *Dragon Fly: Suborder Anisoptera.* 1/2" - 2", large eyes, 6 hooked legs. Wide oval to round abdomen.
18. *Clam: Class Bivalvia.*

GROUP THREE TAXA
Pollution tolerant organisms can be in any quality of water.

19. *Aquatic Worm: Class Oligochaeta.* 1/4" -2", can be very tiny; thin worm-like body.
20. *Midge Fly Larva: Suborder Nematocera.* Up to 1/4", dark head, worm-like segmented body, 2 tiny legs on each side.
21. *Blackfly Larva: Family Simulidae.* Up to 1/4", one end of body wider. Black head, suction pad on end.
22. *Leech: Order Hirudinea.* 1/4" - 2", brown, slimy body, ends with suction pads.
23. *Pouch Snail and Pond Snails: Class Gastropoda.* No operculum. Breathe air. Shell usually opens on left.
24. *Other snails: Class Gastropoda.* No operculum. Breathe air. Snail shell coils in one plane.

Reprinted with permission from:
SAVE OUR STREAMS
Isaak Walton League of America
1401 Wilson Blvd. Level B
Arlington, VA 22209

EarthNotes: Water

"Water represents about 75% of a person's body weight and covers nearly 75% of the earth's surface." (Project Wild, 1987)

Each cubic mile of seawater contains 150 tons of minerals. (Hendrickson, 1984)

If all the ice in the world were melted, the world's oceans would rise 1.7%, or 180 feet. (Hendrickson, 1984)

"Half of the world's population lives less than 6 kilometers from the sea." (Sitarz, 1993)

"Two-thirds of the world's cities with populations of 2.5 million or more are near tidal estuaries." (Sitarz, 1993)

"At least 75% of the fish and shellfish commercially harvested in the ocean are estuary-dependent, but in the Gulf of Mexico, the figure may be as high as 98%." (Council on Environmental Quality, 1992)

"Since colder water contains more oxygen, the ocean that surrounds Antarctica is four times as productive as any other. Hundreds of species of fish, penguins, seals, and whales, and the largest gathering of seabirds in the world thrive there." (Steger & Bowermaster, 1990)

"70 to 80% of water demand worldwide is for agricultural irrigation, less than 20% for industrial use and a mere 6% is for domestic consumption." (Sitarz, 1993)

"Today, some 2.4 billion people in the world live in urban areas. In the industrialized world, most of the urban population are served with water piped into their homes as well as with municipal sanitation services. In contrast, 1.5 billion people in developing countries do not have safe water and over 2 billion lack safe sanitation. By the year 2025, the world's urban population is expected to reach over 5 billion." (Sitarz, 1993)

"An estimated 80% of all diseases and over 1/3 of deaths in developing countries are caused by disease-contaminated water." (Sitarz, 1993)

"Approximately 600,000 tons of oil enter the oceans each year, as a result of normal shipping operations, accidents and illegal discharges." (Sitarz, 1993)

"Each year over 100 million tons of plastic finds its way to the sea, plastic that may not decompose for up to 450 years. The floating, translucent material is often mistaken for prey by birds, turtles, sharks, and fish—they ingest it or get caught in it. More than two million birds and 100,000 sea animals die each year as a result." (Steger & Bowermaster, 1990)

"Most marine species off the Atlantic, Pacific, and Gulf of Mexico coasts are at historically low levels...Recent declines in fish and shellfish are attributable to a combination of overharvesting, bycatch waste, habitat degradation, and introduction of foreign species." (Council on Environmental Quality, 1992)

"28% of the 232 fish groups (representing 450 species) monitored by National Marine Fisheries Service are overharvested." (Council on Environmental Quality, 1992)

"Groundwater is being used much faster than it is being replaced on the assumption that there will always be new sources. 3300 cubic kilometers are withdrawn annually for irrigation purposes: six times the annual flow of the Mississippi River." (Stead & Stead, 1992)

"Unregulated nonpoint sources of pollution, such as runoff from agricultural lands, urban areas, and other types of land uses, account for half of all pollution loadings to coastal waters." (The Council on Environmental Quality, 1992)

"Most people realize there are limits to how much oil can be pumped, but few realize that humanity is also mining a finite reservoir of groundwater. A good example is the rapid depletion of accessible portions of the Ogallala aquifer underlying the Great Plains of the United States. That water accumulated during the last ice age; in some places...where the Ogallala takes in about a half inch of water a year, the water level drops four to six feet annually as pumps empty the aquifer to irrigate cropland. Mining southern parts of the aquifer to economic exhaustion in less than half a century amounts to the greatest overdraft of groundwater in human history. The rate of net withdrawal today is roughly equivalent to the flow of the Colorado River." (Ehrlich & Ehrlich, 1990)

An average of 19 chemical accidents occur each day in the United States, releasing more than 130 million pounds of toxins per year into the environment. A study completed in 1994 by the National Environmental Law Center says that on average two people a day are injured in the chemical accidents. (Associated Press, 1994)

"Once all life was restricted to the sea. Today even man remains linked to it; our body fluids maintain a constant salinity, and proportions of other ingredients in the blood also resemble those of the ocean. Echoes of the rhythms of the sea are found in the reproductive cycles of many land animals, including humans."
— William H. Amos

WATER WITHDRAWALS PER DAY IN THE UNITED STATES

	1940	1990
Total withdrawals	140 billion gallons	408 billion gallons
Per person per day	1,027 gallons	1,620 gallons
Irrigation withdrawals	71 billion gallons	137 billion gallons
Steam for electricity	23 billion gallons	195 billion gallons

(Source: U.S. Bureau of the Census)

John Heine

Going Further: Draw your life like a river.
"Late in the afternoon after we make camp, I ask the group to draw life maps. 'The piece of paper represents your life. Make it as long or short as you want it to be,' I explain. I offer crayons, instructing them to pick colors that feel expressive of their life. 'Now imagine that your life is like the river we're on. Where does the river of you life begin, where are there bends in the shoreline, where is the rapid that threw you out of the boat, where are the languid stretches of flat water, what is the countryside like along your river, where are the eddies that catch you, where is the main current, good campsites, fellow travelers? Draw you life like the river, from beginning to end.

'Let you hand be your guide, and without thinking let the line of your life emerge as a river. Then look over you life, and either by drawing symbols or writing brief narratives, note what specific event is signified by that bend in the river, the rapids, the flat water, the impassable waterfall where you had to get off the river and portage.'" (China Ballard, *Women in the Wilderness*)

Readings: Water

Water must be a basic consideration in everything: forestry, agriculture, and industry. The forest is the mother of the rivers. First we must restore the tree cover to fix the soil, prevent too quick run-off, and steady springs, streams and rivers. We must restore the natural motion of our rivers and, in so doing, we shall restore their vitalizing functions. A river flowing naturally, with its bends, broads and narrows, has the motion of the blood in our arteries, with its inward rotation, tension and relaxation. Picture a river which has risen from a mountain spring in a well-treed watershed...How strange it is that communities fail to realize the importance of preserving tree cover on tree slopes. Man has a bad record as a forest destroyer, cutting and burning greedily and recklessly, destroying the built-up fertility that has accumulated through the centuries. He has been skinning the earth alive in his greed and folly and to satisfy his unnatural appetite for the flesh of his fellow creatures.

—Richard St. Barbe Baker

Water must also be thought of in terms of the chains of life it supports — from the small-as-dust green cells of the drifting plant plankton, through the minute water fleas to the fishes that strain plankton from the water and are in turn eaten by other fishes or by birds, mink, raccoons — in an endless cyclic transfer of materials from life to life. We know that the necessary minerals in the water are so passed from link to link of the food chains. Can we suppose that poisons we introduce into water will not also enter into these cycles of nature?

—Rachel Carson

The river—I remember this like a picture—
the river was the upper twist
of a written question mark.
I know now it takes
many many years to write a river,
a twist of water asking a question.
—Carl Sandburg

And I have loved thee, Ocean! and my joy
Of youthful sports was on thy breast to be
Borne, like thy bubbles, onward: from a boy
I wantoned with thy breakers—they to me
Were a delight; and if the freshening sea
Made them a terror—'twas a pleasing fear,
For I was, as it were, a child of thee,
And trusted to thy billows far and near,
And laid my hand upon thy mane—as I do here.
—Lord Byron

SKY

Sky...

If I could be any animal I think I'd be the hawk that lives on the second peak of Table Rock. God how I love him. How I envy him. He flies alone...The king of all he sees and all he flies above. He's the king of the most beautiful place I've ever seen. He knows only solitude, only that he is, and will always be.
— Outward Bound student, age 18

Without food we could live for weeks and without water for days, but without air we could live only for minutes.

The atmosphere is a blanket of gases surrounding the earth. USSR cosmonaut Vladimir Shatalov said, "When we look into the sky it seems to us to be endless. We breathe without thinking about it, as is natural. We think without consideration about the boundless ocean of air, and then as you sit aboard a spacecraft, you tear away from Earth, and within ten minutes you have been carried straight through the layer of air, and beyond there is nothing! Beyond the air there is only emptiness, coldness, darkness. The 'boundless' blue sky, the ocean which gives breath and protects us from the endless black and death, is but an infinitesimally thin film. How dangerous it is to threaten even the smallest part of this gossamer covering, this conserver of life." (Kelley, 1988)

Three-quarters of the atmosphere lies below the peak of Mount Everest! (Cousteau, 1981)

"Water vapor and airborne particles are essential for the stability of the global ecosystem. Their variations and interactions, combined with the global circulation of the atmosphere, produce the world's weather (including its clouds and precipitation) and are responsible for the blue-green-white appearance of the earth as seen from space." (Schaefer and Day, 1981)

The layer of air in relation to the size of the earth has been compared to the skin of an apple. Within this relatively thin layer are several other layers: the troposphere, where our weather takes place, is the seven miles more or less (more at the equator, less at the poles) which contains most of the atmosphere and most of our weather. The stratosphere contains the ozone layer that absorbs life-damaging ultraviolet rays, thus making life as we know it possible on Earth. If the ozone in the stratosphere was "compressed into a liquid layer over the globe at sea level, it would have a thickness of less than 3/16th of an inch." (Schaefer & Day, 1981)

The different shades of blue in the air, the sunlight and shadows, the colors and textures of the clouds, the glorious sunsets and less often seen glorious sunrises, the life-giving rays of the sun, the beauty of the moon and stars, the variety of pressures and humidities, the rains from light mists to cold drizzles to hot heavy drops to thick downpours, snow and hail, lightning, thunder, haze and fog, crystal clear days, stillnesses, light breaths of wind, cool breezes, frenzied blasts of air, days that feel perfect, days of almost unbearable heat and brittle cold, the changes of seasons, the airborne seeds—these are all gifts from the sky.

If the stars should appear one night in a thousand years, how would men believe and adore; and preserve for many generations the remembrance of the city of God which had been shown! But every night come out these envoys of beauty, and light the universe with their admonishing smile.

Standing on the bare ground,—my head bathed by the blithe air, and uplifted into infinite space,—all mean egotism vanishes. I become a transparent eye-ball; I am nothing; I see all; the currents of the Universal Being circulate through me; I am part or particle of God.

Both quotes are from "Nature"
by Ralph Waldo Emerson

Talking About The Weather

Time Required	A few minutes daily
Group Size	Any
Materials	Writing and drawing materials; weather-monitoring equipment
Location	Anywhere
Indoor Use	Yes
Intended Result	Knowledge of and connections to everyday weather

SUMMARY: Students keep a weather journal.

PROCEDURE: Start a weather journal or have students keep weather journals individually or in teams. We spend too much time being unaware of what's happening in the air around us and the sky above us. Establish times of day for measurements. If possible, measure several times throughout the day.
— Include: Temperature — What are today's high, low? Pressure — How did it change? Did it indicate the day's weather? Wind direction and speed — Did it change during the day? From what direction(s) did it come? What was the wind chill factor? Precipitation — What form did it take? Accumulation — How much was there? Also: Relative humidity, Cloud types, Rising and setting times of sun and moon, Phase of moon, Tides, Seasonal norms.
— Compare with: Other latitudes, other altitudes.
— Pay attention to: Animal behavior, insect sounds, smells.

Throughout my childhood I kept meticulous weather logs; every day I would record the high and the low temperatures, note the cloud cover and any noteworthy events. I kept that up through high school, eventually collecting my own recording instruments. Those hours spent monitoring the skies taught me a lot about the weather and have literally saved my life during my explorations, when I've been trapped in snowstorms thousands of miles from the nearest weatherman.

— Will Steger

FOLLOW-UP:

1. Use Schaefer and Day's Field Guide to the Atmosphere or another weather guide to take your studies further.
2. Draw the clouds. Be creative or realistic. Use pencil, pen, crayon, or watercolors.
3. Write rain poems and songs.

> The day settled down so softly and lovingly upon the earth, touching everything, filling everthing. The sky visibly came down. You could see it among the trees and between the hills. The sun poured himself into the earth as into a cup, and the atmosphere fairly swam with warmth and light.
>
> —John Burroughs

Our Atmosphere

Time Required	20 minutes
Group Size	6-12
Materials	Candle, bottle, tarp
Location-Act.'s 1 & 2	On the trail
Location-Discussion	Anywhere
Indoor Use	Yes
Intended Result	Awareness that the atmosphere is both finite and vulnerable

ACTIVITY 1

SUMMARY: A candle under a jar uses up its oxygen supply, demonstrating the result of a closed system.

PREPARATION: Set up tarp with low sides like a tent for Activities 1 and 2.

PROCEDURE: Everyone gets under the tarp Light the candle and talk about how it, like we, needs oxygen to survive. Put the jar over the candle and watch it use up its supply of oxygen.

ACTIVITY 2

DESCRIPTION: As the group spends time beneath the tarp, the air quality changes and deteriorates.

PROCEDURE: Use Activity 1 as a lead-in. Talk about life under the tarp. There are oxygen users here, carbon dioxide producers, but there are no oxygen producers. The air begins to get a little stuffy. Explain that as the oxygen supply is diminished, the quality of life, energy, and thought declines.

> For the first time in my life I saw the horizon as a curved line. It was accentuated by a thin seam of dark blue light—our atmosphere. Obviously this was not the ocean of air I had been told it was so many times in my life. I was terrified by its fragile appearance.
> —Ulf Merbold, astronaut,
> Federal Republic of Germany

If we were to light a small fire under the tarp, we would have to share our oxygen with it. Of course the tarp is not airtight and oxygen is coming in from outside, and everyone can leave the tarp and solve the immediate problem. Explain that to make life under the tarp a closed system would demonstrate the point better, but would be dangerous. Let the group rearrange the tarp for better airflow or let everyone move outside.

FOLLOW-UP: Explain that the planet is ultimately a closed system. If in using oxygen and producing carbon dioxide we use more oxygen than our system can produce, then we change the quality of life. What can we do to keep replenishing the world's oxygen?

VARIATION: Indoors, students can explore how the classroom gets air. Are the windows used? If so, for how much of the year? Tour your school's ventilation system, learn how the air circulates into and out of the building. Discuss what would happen if the ventilation system failed to work and all of the windows and doors were shut. How many plants are there in the school that could contribute to the oxygen supply? Remind the students that the planet is a closed system and that clean air is one of the prime necessities of life. The planet generates oxygen—humans must now make an effort to make sure that the supply of fresh air does not decline.

John Heine

WHAT IS THE GREENHOUSE EFFECT?

Over the last fifteen years, scientists have closely monitored the earth's atmosphere. Their objective: to determine whether industrial processes affect the world's temperature. Their conclusion: the planet is moving into the early stages of an unprecedented shift in climate—a global warming trend of alarming proportions. If left unchecked, this global warming trend will adversely affect all life on earth. This global warming is called the "greenhouse effect."

Throughout much of the earth's history there has been a natural greenhouse effect. Certain gases have always formed a blanket around the earth. This greenhouse blanket allows the sun's rays to pass through to the surface of the earth, while absorbing some of the reflected heat energy. This trapped heat insulates the earth, providing a warm temperature bank that stimulates the life process. Without this natural heat shield, the earth would be a cold, lifeless planet. But now, various industrial gases are thickening the greenhouse blanket, which is trapping more and more heat around the planet.

Many scientists predict that if current trends in greenhouse pollution continue, industrial activities will subject the globe to a temperature rise of four to nine degrees Fahrenheit in the next seven decades. By comparison, the average global temperature has not varied more than 3.6 degrees Fahrenheit in the 18,000 years during which human civilization has emerged. A temperature climb of four to nine degrees would exceed the entire increase in global temperatures since the end of the last Ice Age.

The buildup of greenhouse gases will radically affect temperatures, rainfall patterns, agricultural productivity, and natural ecosystems throughout the world. "We may be moving through an entire geological epoch in a single century...changing the entire fabric of nature," states John Hoffman, director of the global atmosphere program at the Environmental Protection Agency (EPA).

CARBON DIOXIDE. About 50% of the greenhouse effect is caused by atmospheric increases in carbon dioxide. Since the advent of the industrial revolution, manmade CO_2 emission has increased by 5,300%. Every year 5.5 billion tons of CO_2 are added to the Earth's atmosphere. In the United States we generate about six tons of CO_2 a year per person. This results primarily when fossil fuels such as coal, oil, and natural gas are burned to run our power plants, homes, automobiles, and factories.

CHLOROFLUOROCARBONS (CFCs) represent the cause of approximately 15 to 20% of the greenhouse effect. CFCs are industrial chemicals widely used in air conditioners, refrigerators, solvents, plastic packaging, and foam insulation. Many CFCs hold heat in the atmosphere at a rate several thousand times more than CO_2 particles, and remain in the atmosphere for over 100 years.

METHANE comprises approximately 18% of all greenhouse gases. Methane is produced by cattle, rice fields, and is also emitted by landfills when organic waste breaks down.

NITROUS OXIDES account for approximately 10% of the greenhouse effect. They are formed by the burning of fossil fuels, natural microbial activity in the soil, and the breakdown of chemical fertilizers.

OZONE, in the stratosphere, is a vital atmospheric component. But at ground level, ozone is a lung irritant and pollutant which accounts for about 5% of the greenhouse effect. Ozone comes from the ground-based pollution created by motor vehicles, power plants and oil refineries.

Though the United States has only 5% of the world's population, we contribute 26% of the world's carbon dioxide and 27% of the world's CFCs.

But most men, it seems to me, do not care for Nature and would sell their share in all her beauty, as long as they may live, for a stated sum—many for a glass of rum. Thank God, men cannot as yet fly, and lay waste to the sky as well as the earth! We are safe on that side for the present. It is for the very reason that some do not care for those things that we need to continue to protect all from the vandalism of a few.

—Henry David Thoreau

WHAT IS OZONE DEPLETION?

The ozone in the upper atmosphere provides a vital shield which prevents hazardous ultraviolet radiation emitted by the sun from reaching the earth. Now, though, emission of CFCs is destroying the ozone shield. CFCs migrate to the upper atmosphere where they're broken down by the sun's rays. This process releases particles of chlorine, which in turn destroy the ozone layer.

The National Aeronautics and Space Administration (NASA) predicts the ozone layer will decrease by 10% by the year 2050. An ozone loss of this magnitude would expose the earth to dangerous levels of ultraviolet radiation. The EPA predicts hundreds of millions of cases of skin cancer over the next decades if ozone depletion goes unchecked. Increases in ultraviolet radiation also damage the immune system, making humans and the rest of the animal kingdom susceptible to a host of new diseases. Plant species are also vulnerable to ultraviolet radiation. A 15% reduction in stratospheric ozone could cause crop losses of $2.6 billion a year in the United States.

WHAT IS ACID RAIN?

Pollution from coal-burning power plants, factories, homes, automobiles, and trucks is decimating forests around the world. The burning of coal releases sulphur dioxide and nitrous oxides. When released into the atmosphere, these gases produce acid rain. By 1984, 50% of forests in West Germany had been damaged by acid rain. In many other European countries, 25 to 50% of forests have been severely damaged by acid rain.

In the United States, many lakes in the Northeast have experienced devastating reductions in fish life because of increased acidity. Acid rain is also damaging the earth's soil, causing a ten-fold increase in soil acidity in some countries over the past 60 years.

Recent research also indicates that acid rain prevents soil microbes from consuming methane, a leading greenhouse gas. Thus, acid rain contributes to the greenhouse effect. The total financial losses each year to acid rain are staggering. The yearly worldwide damage to crops, forests, lakes, and buildings is in the tens of billions of dollars.

Individual consumer choices can reduce problems associated with the Greenhouse Effect, Ozone Depletion, and Acid Rain. See *50 Things You Can Do To Save the Earth* and similar books for specific actions.

Going Further:
Individuals, groups, or classes can measure the acidity of local rainfall. See *Saving the Earth* (Steger & Bowermaster, 1990), page 88 for instructions.

Choosing The Future

Time Required	30 minutes or longer
Group size	Any
Materials	Copies of choices
Location	Anywhere
Indoor Use	Yes, also Variation
Intended Result	Recognition of the complexity of working to solve environmental problems

SUMMARY: The group experiences the difficulties which leaders face as they make environmental choices.

PREPARATION: Make copies of options with which the group will grapple. Add your own. The purposes of this activity are to raise awareness of the issues, communicate the complexity of decision making, and emphasize the need for cooperation—so extensive background knowledge of the issues is not necessary. (But see Classroom Variation below.)

PROCEDURE: Tell the group that they are the Environmental Committee of a state legislature. Six bills and issues related to the environment have come before the Committee. Every "no" vote on the following six proposals is pro-conservation; every yes vote is pro-development, The House Speaker, Senate President, and Governor will accept your recommendations as long as you decide unanimously on three no and three yes votes. If you fail to reach consensus in the allotted time, the bills move to the House and Senate floor where four to six bills will certainly be passed by pro-development forces. (Some might argue that the pro-conservation votes should be "Yes" instead of "No" votes. Often, however, laws and issues are worded and considered so that the pro-conservation vote is viewed as negative. Unlike most legislative committees, however, exercise participants are probably pro-conservation, for this reason trade-offs of pro-development for pro-conservation votes and unanimity have been introduced to help participants grapple with complexity.)

Each committee member briefs herself for five minutes before the meeting begins. Then the Committee must make its choices during the next 25 minutes, at which point all matters will be referred to the legislature.

THE OPTIONS:
1. The wood chip industry wants to come to your state. If they come, they will clearcut all old growth forests and 50% of all other hardwood forests in your state over the next 10 years. They will also bring money to your

state's forest landowners. The chips will be shipped overseas to be used in particle board, plywood, wrapping and tissue paper. To permit the building of the wood chip plants, vote yes.

2. Most of the state's electricity is supplied by a high sulfur content coal-fired power plant. The utility says it cannot afford scrubbers to clean the plant's emissions but wants to spend much more money on the construction of a nuclear power plant. The nuclear facility will not pollute the air during normal operation but will have to store its used radioactive waste on site. Environmentalists argue that a combination of scrubbers and conservation are cheaper and more appropriate. To allow the construction of the nuclear power plant, vote yes.

3. Air quality in your state's urban areas is among the worst in the country due to auto emissions. Use of public transportation would greatly reduce emissions. Financing the public transportation would mean increasing state sales tax from 4% to 5%, a 20% increase. Your committee is the last hurdle for the sales tax increase. Senior citizens, merchants, and many other citizens have come up with a proposal to reject the tax increase. To kill the increase and reject public transportation, vote yes.

4. A new Air Force base will bring 10,000 jobs to your state, strengthening business activity by $100 million per year. There would be significant noise and air pollution due to hundreds of take-offs and landings of experimental aircraft. Further, the base will destroy an ecologically sensitive area of 25 square miles and seriously impact another 50 square miles. To approve the construction of the Air Force base, vote yes.

5. The state school system has been mandated to produce an environmental education curriculum for all students from kindergarten through 12th grade. Since this curriculum calls for annual field trips for every student as well as outdoor and experiential education, it is quite expensive. It was originally thought the education budget was adequate, but an influx of population and unexpected building, repair, and administrative costs have left no money for the curriculum. A new property tax is needed to finance the curriculum. Your committee is the last hurdle to that financing. A coalition of business, industry, and citizens' groups opposes any property tax increases, and that coalition has gotten a proposal to your committee. Vote yes to kill the tax increase and stop the environmental education curriculum.

6. The water works board of your state's largest city has purchased land where the last two free-flowing rivers in the state come together. They plan to build a reservoir to guarantee their water supply. Environmentalists argue that water conservation make the reservoir unnecessary. Furthermore, some environmentally sensitive areas will be flooded. The business community is firmly behind building the reservoir. While all of

the issues have some political implications, this one has become especially volatile. A vote for the water works board is politically astute but environmentally risky. A vote against the reservoir may be political suicide. Vote yes to allow the building of the reservoir.

FOLLOW-UP: Discuss how individuals made their choices and how the group reached consensus.

VARIATION, Classroom: After discussing the issues, students could choose one that especially interested them and research it. After presentations the committee could convene again to see if its decisions would be any different.

Go Flying

Time Required	30 minutes or more
Group size	Any
Materials	Flying machine materials
Location	Outdoors /Indoors
Indoor Use	Yes
Intended Result	First-hand knowledge of the ocean of air

SUMMARY: Various activities involve the use of kites and gliders to emphasize that the air is not empty, that the air is a medium.

PREPARATION: If you intend to make kites for flying, then research kite designs and obtain appropriate materials. Knowledge of wind and weather patterns for your area will help with some activities.

There are many sources for simple kite plans, among them James Wagenvoord's *Flying Kites* (The Macmillan Company, New York, 1968); *Flying, Gliding, and Whirling* by Carol Nicklaus (Franklin Watts, New York, 1981); and *Kites and Other Wind Machines* by Andre Thiebault (Sterling Publishing Co., New York, 1982)—this last one has very simple kites, including a strip of paper folded around into a funnel with the two ends of the paper hanging down as tails and the kite string attached to the top of the funnel.

PROCEDURE:

ACTIVITY #1: On a windy day, bring out different kinds of store-bought or handmade kites—paper and wood, plastic, beach kites, styrofoam disk. Which will fly better where you are? Why? Beach kites, for example, are designed for constant winds and don't usually fly well inland. Why is the air different at the coast from inland? Which direction is the wind coming from; what can that mean for your weather?

ACTIVITY #2: Build your own kites with paper, string, tape, and cloth. Have small groups build kites together. Test them.

ACTIVITY #3: Human kites. In an open area, preferably on a hillside, have one person fly the "kite." She will let out and take in the string, pull or direct the "kite." The "kite" itself can be from one to four people who respond to the flyer and to the wind. The "kite" can experiment with swaying, looping, being carried in a direction by the real gusts of wind. When one person is the kite, she can close her eyes or be blindfolded to help her focus on feeling the wind. When the kite is two or more people, they hold onto each other and must respond together to the kite string and the wind—the more people who make up the kite, the harder it is for them to coordinate.

ACTIVITY #4(Classroom): Decorate kites for a classroom display where the kites, individualized by the students, seem to be zooming above the heads of the class. What are the best months to fly a kite? What are the worst? Why? What are good kite stories that have happened to people in the class? What are good kite stories students can make up? What are good kite stories students can make up from the viewpoint of the kite? Write stories on the kites themselves before hanging them.

ACTIVITY #5: Build paper airplanes and decorate them. Compare their performance against store-bought gliders under different circumstances. Have the students decorate the gliders to look like flying things—birds and flying squirrels and bats and flying machines and seeds with wings. See who can fly gliders further, higher, most accurately. See whose shows the least wear and tear.

FOLLOW-UP: Emphasize that aerodynamics depends on the air, which is not an invisible nothing but an invisible something.

It's difficult to be self-conscious when your eyes are fixed on a kite moving with the wind and the sky. It's a lot easier just to let a smile happen.

—James Wagenvoord

EarthNotes: Sky

"The very composition of the atmosphere—the oxygen-rich air that animals breathe—is a result of the activities of organisms, primarily green plants, over eons of Earth's history. Nonhuman organisms are still active in maintaining a favorable balance of atmospheric gases." (Ehrlich & Ehrlich, 1990)

"According to the U.S. Environmental Protection Agency, an estimated 110 million Americans—nearly half the country—live in areas with levels of air pollution the federal government considers to be harmful...Most of the problem, says EPA, has to do with cars." (Makower, 1992)

"Researchers sampled air quality in 12 national parks twice a week from 1982 to 1992. Their results were published in the March [1994] issue of the *Atmospheric Environment Journal.* Over the 10-year period, summer haze soared 39% in the Great Smoky Mountains National Park in Tennessee and 37% in Virginia's Shenandoah National Park. In other words, if visitors to the Great Smoky park could see 12 miles away in 1982, they could see only 8 miles away in 1992. Summertime sulfate concentrations in the air at those two parks exceeded levels found in Los Angeles.
(Associated Press, 5/28/94.)

"Carbon dioxide in the United States is emitted at a rate of five tons per person per year, which is five times the world's average per capita rate." (Stead & Stead, 1992)

Between 1975 and 1989 the United States reduced ambient levels of the following six key air pollutants—"criteria" pollutants for which the federal government has established health-based air quality standards:

Lead	93% reduction
Carbon monoxide	47% reduction
Ozone	14% reduction
Particulate matter	20% reduction
Nitrogen oxide	17% reduction
Sulfur dioxide	46% reduction

(Source: US EPA, quoted by Council on Environmental Quality, 1992)

Readings: Sky

Our fantastic civilization has fallen out of touch with many aspects of nature, and with none more completely than with night...With lights and ever more lights, we drive the holiness and beauty of night back to the forests and the sea...Are modern folk, perhaps, afraid of night? Do they fear the vast serenity, the mystery of infinite space, the austerity of stars? Having made themselves at home in a civilization obsessed with power, which explains its whole world in terms of energy, do they fear at night for their dull acquiescence and the pattern of their beliefs? Be the answer what it will, today's civilization is full of people who have not the slightest notion of the character or the poetry of the night, who have never even seen night. Yet to live thus, to know only artificial night, is as absurd and evil as to know only artificial day.
> —Henry Beston

> Men say they know many things;
> But lo! they have taken wings, —
> The arts and sciences,
> And a thousand appliances;
> The wind that blows
> Is all that anybody knows.
> > —Henry David Thoreau

Air pollution is not merely a nuisance and a threat to health. It is a reminder that our most celebrated technological achievements—the automobile, the jet plane, the power plant, industry in general, and indeed the modern city itself—are, in the environment, failures.
> —Barry Commoner

I'm an explorer and an environmentalist, not a preacher. But it should be obvious to everyone that these problems won't reverse themselves on their own. Government, industry, and individuals must step in and take responsibility...It is difficult to comprehend that when you do a simple chore like changing the Freon in your car's air conditioner, you are helping to destroy the ozone layer that shields the planet. But it is essential to remind yourself every day that people—you and I—are causing all this destruction; there is no one else to blame.
> —Will Steger

Nest Eggs

Birds all the sunny day
Flutter and quarrel
Here in the arbour-like
Tent of the laurel.
Here in the fork
The brown nest is seated;
Four little blue eggs
The mother keeps heated...
Soon the frail eggs they shall
Chip, and upspringing,
Make all the April woods
Merry with singing.
Younger than we are,
O children, and frailer,
Soon in blue air they'll be
Singer and sailor.
We so much older,
Taller and stronger,
We shall look down on the
Birdies no longer.
They shall go flying
With musical speeches
High overhead in the
Tops of the beeches.
In spite of our wisdom
And sensible talking,
We on our feet must go
Plodding and walking.

—Robert Louis Stevenson

FIRE

Fire...

The feeling that I have now is one of a gigantic spark that has ignited a wildfire.
           —17 year old Outward Bound student

Fire gives us light and warmth, heat and comfort, energy and beauty. Fire is the spark that makes life possible.

Energy surrounds us. We contain it, and we use the energy in other things, animate and inanimate, to make our lives fuller and easier.

The main physical source of fire is, for us, the sun. Solar energy, wind energy, water energy, the energy in food, in oil, in coal, all come from the sun. The fire of the sun gives us our transportation, the heat of woodfire and furnace, the light of flashlight, streetlight, and computer.

We stare into the flames of a campfire, into its coals—its heat and light touch us and we feel a connection we can't fathom. We light our stoves and cook our dinner and brew our beverage; and we eat and drink the warmth as well as the food.

The rest of the natural world uses solar energy more directly than humans do. All other plants and animals use the sun's energy either directly or as biomass. Only we mine stored solar energy in the form of oil, coal, and gas. We have spoiled huge areas of pristine beauty to obtain these materials. We are polluting the world by burning its solar preserves. We continue to use fuel as though its supplies are unending. We have become addicted to it. What will we do as fuel continues to cost more to extract? What will we do as we use it up?

Sometimes we bask in the sunlight, feeding our skins the light and heat of the sun. We see the sun's life-giving properties reflected in the moon, mirrored in the other stars, echoed in our campfires, transformed in our transportation and appliances. We must nurture the fire, use what we need, save what we can.

Running On Empty

Time Required	10 minutes or longer
Group size	10 or more
Materials	Stopwatch or timer
Location	Open area
Indoor Use	Yes
Intended Result	Awareness of energy efficiency issues

SUMMARY: Using "energy units" in competition, teams learn about energy efficiencies and inefficiencies.

PROCEDURE: Divide the group into teams of 5-10 people. Each team will be given a number of "energy points" and rules for their use. Teams will compete to complete tasks (see below) using the energy units. If teams have different numbers of members, calculate energy used per person.

Encourage creativity. The point system refers to the activity of one person touching the ground. Certain group action might be similar to mass transit or carpooling.

One says to me, "I wonder that you do not lay up money; you love to travel; you might take the cars and go to Fitchburg to-day and see the country." But I am wiser than that. I have learned that the swiftest traveller is he that goes afoot. I say to my friend, Suppose we try who will get there first. The distance is thirty miles; the fare ninety cents. That is almost a day's wages. I remember when wages were sixty cents a day for laborers on this very road. Well, I start now on foot, and get there before night; I have travelled at that rate by the week together. You will in the mean while have earned your fare, and arrive there some time to-morrow, or possibly this evening, if you are lucky enough to get a job in season. Instead of going to Fitchburg, you will be working here the greater part of the day. And so, if the railroad reached round the world, I think that I should keep ahead of you; and as for seeing the country and getting experience of that kind, I should have to cut your acquaintance altogether.
— Henry David Thoreau

ENERGY UNIT POINTS

Heel/toe — 1

Roll 360 degrees lying down — 4

Normal step — 5

Commando crawl — 5

Hop on one foot — 8

Skip — 10

One gallop — 8

Giant step — 12

Running step — 15

Forward roll — 15

Long jump — 20

Cartwheel — 20

TASKS:

1. Give each team 100 (50, 200) energy units. Using the energy unit point system, ask the teams to figure out how to get maximum efficiency from their energy. Let them practice for five minutes, then see who can go the farthest.
2. Give each team an equal distance to cover. Which team can get there using the least number of units?
3. Give each team an equal distance to cover but ask them to do it as fast as possible. Who can get there the fastest? How did the number of energy units used compare between Tasks 2 and 3.

VARIATIONS:Create your own point system, contests, modes of transportation. Let your students help invent them to give the students ownership.

> The typical American male devotes more than 1,600 hours a year to his car. He sits in it while it goes and while it stands idling. He parks it and searches for it. He earns the money to put down on it and to meet the monthly installments. He works to pay for petrol, tolls, insurance, taxes, and tickets. He spends four of his sixteen waking hours on the road or gathering his resources for it. The model American puts in 1,600 hours to get 7,500 miles: less than five miles per hour. In countries deprived of a transportation industry, people manage to do the same, walking wherever they want to go.
> —Ivan Illich

The following energy facts were compiled by EarthSave (*Earthsave*, Spring/Summer 1991):

—If every nation expended as much oil per person in agriculture as does the US, current world oil reserves would be emptied in 12 years. (*Gaia, An Atlas of Planet Management*, Myers, Norman,General Editor, Doubleday, p. 65, 1984)

—North America possesses only 4% of proven global oil reserves. At our current rate of oil use, these native resources would last only ten more years. (MacKenzie, James J., "Why We Need a National Energy Policy," *World Resources Institute in Focus*, Spring 1991, Carrying Capacity Network, Washington, D.C.)

—U.S. oil production is falling in Alaska and the 48 states and is likely to continue to fall in the U.S. We are importing almost 50% of our oil. (Ibid.)

—In 1985, there was a 280% increase in drilling compared to 1973, yet more oil was produced in 1973 than in 1985. (Ibid.)

—While the fuel consumed per vehicle in the United States has dropped 15% since 1970, total motor-vehicle use is up 40% and the total number of motor vehicles has increased by 70%. (Ibid.)

Fire Building

Time Required	30 minutes or longer
Group size	Any
Materials	Tinder, wood, matches, firepan
Location	Outdoors
Indoor Use	No
Intended Result	Ability to build a low impact, no-trace fire

SUMMARY: Students learn to build a one match fire and a no-trace fire.

PROCEDURE: Remind students that fire building is a useful skill which uses a renewable available source of energy. Fires do, however, have environmental impact and must be used responsibly. Discuss the pros and cons of fires, and compare fires to cooking with petroleum-based fuels. Let the group build a no-trace fire, make a hot drink, put out their fire, and leave no trace.

TINDER—Have each person gather one or two types of tinder. Burn each type one at a time and compare: How quickly does it burn? How long does it last? Talk about ways to dry tinder (in pockets or hats, off the ground). Some types to look for include pine pitch, spruce pitch, yellow and river birch bark, hemlock hair, dry grasses. Of course, no living material should be used.

WOOD—Collection of materials is critical in fire building. Find dry wood, generally from non-standing trees. Listen when the wood snaps—usually the higher the pitch the dryer the wood. Notice the sound of different woods when they break. Organize wood by sizes into tinder, tiny fuel (match stick size and smaller), pencil-sized, and finger-sized. No wood should be larger than wrist sized.

NO-TRACE FIRE—Dig a 15-inch diameter circle in order to lift out topsoil in one plug. Cut all around with a shovel, place finger size strong branches underneath and lift. Set it aside. Place dirt around the edge of the hole to protect plants, and remove flammable materials within 6 feet of the fire pit. Burn wood completely and scatter dead ashes. Heal the site and do your best to make it look as if no fire had ever been there.

FIRE PAN—A "no-trace" fire is certainly not the same as a no-damage fire. Consider carrying along a fire pan, such as a charcoal grill without the legs. Mount it solidly on a few rocks and you've got the easiest campfire base with the least impact.

VARIATION—ORGANIC BASE FIRE: This fire tests whether you've done the job of protecting the earth's surface. These instructions, by Brett M. Bloomston, appeared in Issue #12 of the *Bankhead Monitor* and are used with permission.

MATERIALS NEEDED: several large slabs of tree bark, a few pounds of loose soil, wood to burn, and one green leaf.

STEP 1: Clear a place for the fire and lay the leaf in the center of the clearing. The leaf serves as a test to see if your base has protected the earth.

STEP 2: Place the tree bark "cradle-up" and cover the entire ground by overlapping the pieces. Remember to build your base much larger than you anticipate the fire's size to be. (Make sure you only take bark from fallen trees. Peeling bark from a live tree is a deadly flesh-wound to our deciduous friends.)

STEP 3: Cover the tree bark with at least two inches of loose soil. Make sure the soil is not from a trail (this leads to erosion) and does not have rocks in it. The best place to find such soil is the uprooted base of a fallen tree.

STEP 4: Build your fire and enjoy.

STEP 5: When the fire is cool and you are positive that no coals remain, spread the ashes in surrounding vegetation.

STEP 6: Check your green leaf. If it is still green after your fire has died, then the ground was protected from the fire.

NOTE: Other firebuilding exercises use a tarp instead of a leaf—the tarp offers an added layer of protection for the ground. If you build your fire incorrectly you ruin the tarp.

Of course, you can consider building no fire at all. Instead of a campfire, try a camp-flame, a lantern or candle that people can sit around while they talk into the night.

Solar Stills

Time Required	2 hours or longer
Group size	Any
Materials	Large pot, small cup, plastic, tape, small rock, dirty water
Location	Outdoors or in strong sunlight
Indoor Use	Yes
Intended Result	Understanding of how solar stills work

SUMMARY: Students make a solar still.

PREPARATION: Gather materials

PROCEDURE: These directions can be followed by small groups or by individuals: Put a 1 to 1-1/2 inch layer of dirty or brackish water in the pot. Place the cup in the center of the pot. Cover the top of the pot with a layer of plastic which folds over the sides, then tape or otherwise attach the plastic to the sides of the pot. Place a small rock in the center of the plastic so that water will be able to run down the inside of the plastic sheet into the cup.

Presto: you've created a solar still. Place in strong sunlight. Water drops will begin to form on the underside of the plastic sheet within half an hour. After several hours in the sun, water will have dripped into the cup.

FOLLOW-UP: Discuss what happened to the water. What kind of water is in the cup? What is the residue left in the bottom of the pot? What implications do solar stills have for people?

VARIATIONS:
1. Place different stills in varying amounts of sunlight and shade to see how much faster evaporation and condensation take place.
2. An outdoor solar still can be built on the trail but will require a hole two to three feet in diameter and a foot and a half deep. The plastic is stretched over the entire hole and weighted with rocks all around. Water from the soil will condense on the underside of the plastic sheet and will flow into the pot.

Going Further: Build a Solar Oven.
The Problem: Seventy percent of people in developing countries use wood for fuel, as much as 90% of that for cooking. The United Nations Food and Agriculture Organization "estimates that in 1980, around 1.3 billion people

lived in wood-deficit areas. If this population-driven overharvesting continues at present rates, by the year 2000 some 2.4 billion people may be living
in areas where wood is acutely scarce." (The Brundtland Report, 1987)

Remember, too, that "An estimated 80% of all diseases and over 1/3
of deaths in developing countries are caused by disease-contaminated
water." (Sitarz, 1993)

Wood shortage also means that forests are stripped bare, destroying
diversity and contributing to erosion and flooding. In many cases people
burn manure as an alternative to wood—the manure would be better used
to fertilize soil. Others are forced to spend up to 30% of income on cooking
fuel alone.

The Solution: These problems can be greatly alleviated by solar ovens.
Solar ovens are inexpensive, relatively easy to construct, and work in most
parts of the world.

What You Can Do: You or your students can build solar ovens, experiment with them, and use them in demonstration and education projects.
The ovens both cook food and distill water. For more information on solar
ovens, including plans, write Solar Cookers International—see appendix for
address.

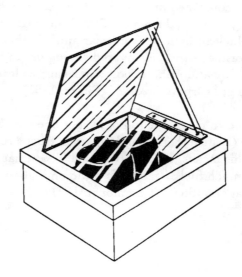

(Illustration from *The Solar Box Cooker Manual*, from Solar Cookers
International. Used with permission.)

EarthNotes: Fire

From the Brundtland Report

"A safe and sustainable energy pathway is crucial to sustainable development; we have not yet found it."

"Today the average person in an industrial market economy uses more than 80 times as much energy as someone in sub-Saharan Africa."

"To bring developing countries' energy use up to industrialized country levels by the year 2025 would require increasing present global energy use by a factor of five. The planetary ecosystem could not stand this, especially if the increases were based on non-renewable fossil fuels. Threats of global warming and acidification of the environment most probably rule out even a doubling of energy use based on present mixes of primary sources."

"Energy efficiency can only buy time for the world to develop 'low-energy paths' based on renewable sources, which should form the foundation of the global energy structure during the 21st century."

"The amount of energy that goes into feeding the average American for one day (all of the oil, gas, chemicals, etc.) totals about 250,000 calories." (Stead & Stead, 1992)

"Most of the energy consumed on this planet comes from fossil fuels. 40% of the world's energy is derived from oil, 30% from coal or wood, and 20% from natural gas. Nuclear, hydropower, solar and all other sources supply less than 10% of world energy. This overwhelming use of fossil fuel is a significant source of many atmospheric pollutants such as lead, sulfur dioxide and the greenhouse gas carbon dioxide." (Sitarz, 1993)

"The energy required to move one ton of freight one mile by rail now averages about 624 btu (British thermal units), while trucks require about 3,460 btu per ton mile. This means that, for the same freight haulage, trucks burn nearly six times as much fuel as railroads—and emit about six times as much environmental pollution." (Commoner, 1971)

Readings: Fire

A people can be just as dangerously overpowered by the wattage of its tools as by the caloric content of its foods, but it is much harder to confess to a national overindulgence in wattage than to a sickening diet.
          —Ivan Illich

We had a remarkable sunset one day last November. I was walking in a meadow, the source of a small brook, when the sun at last, just before setting, after a cold gray day, reached a clear stratum in the horizon, and the softest, brightest morning sunlight fell on the dry grass and on the stems of the trees in the opposite horizon, and on the leaves of the shrub-oaks on the hill-side, while our shadows stretched long over the meadow eastward, as if we were the only motes in its beams. It was such a light as we could not have imagined a moment before, and the air also was so warm and serene that nothing was wanting to make a paradise of that meadow. When we reflected that this was not a solitary phenomenon, never to happen again, but that it would happen forever and ever an infinite number of evenings, and cheer and reassure the latest child that walked there, it was more glorious still.
          —Henry David Thoreau

The ultimate work of energy production is accomplished not in any specialized organ but in every cell of the body. A living cell, like a flame, burns fuel to produce the energy on which life depends. The analogy is more poetic than precise, for the cell accomplishes its 'burning' with only the moderate heat of the body's normal temperature. Yet all these billions of gently burning little fires spark the energy of life. Should they cease to burn, "no heart could beat, no plant could grow upward defying gravity, no amoeba could swim, no sensation could speed along a nerve, no thought could flash in the human brain," said the chemist Eugene Rabinowitch.
          —Rachel Carson

Notes:

THE LIVING WORLD

The Living World...

I have learned to love the earth more now than I have ever loved it and if I could give just one bit of advice I would say to everyone: every day you should hug a person and hug a tree. —19 year old Outward Bound student

Land, Water, Sky, Fire, the non-living elements of our unique blue planet, in themselves set Earth apart from anything else in the known universe. What makes Earth even more wonderful is its possession of the complex and amazing world of plants and animals. The plant kingdom is a vast array of living, breathing entities: plants encompass everything from photosynthesizers on Caribbean reefs to redwoods in California, from rhododendrons in the mountain hollows of North Carolina to reindeer moss growing on the Arctic tundra.

And we animals depend on the plants, directly and indirectly, for our existence. Animals, too, exist in multitudinous forms. Our mobility has given us advantages over plants, and we are able to range through a broad arena of altitude and climate.

There is much to think about and much to celebrate in the animal kingdom. While humans appear to have more complex mental operations than other animals, we are not the fastest, the strongest, the most agile, or the most skillful in seeing, hearing, tasting, smelling or feeling. The animal kingdom offers examples of tenacity, courage, patience, generosity, and endurance that inspire and enrich our lives.

If we tried to catalog the uses of animals and plants to humans, the list would go on and on. But we have to appreciate our fellow beings not merely because of their usefulness to us but simply because we are here together. John Muir had this to say about poison ivy:

Poison oak or poison ivy, both as a bush and a scrambler up trees and rocks, is common throughout the foothill region...It is somewhat troublesome to most travelers, inflaming the skin and eyes, but blends harmoniously with its companion plants, and many a charming flower leans confidingly upon it for protection and shade...Sheep eat it without apparent ill effects; so do horses to some extent, though not fond of it, and to many persons it is harmless. Like most other things not apparently useful to man, it has few friends, and the blind question, "Why was it made?" goes on and on with never a guess that first of all it might have been made for itself.

"Without the beasts," said Chief Seattle, "men would die from a great loneliness of spirit." We must be mindful of our actions and their effects on the living world.

The following activities help participants appreciate the **Living World**; they also offer ways in which we can work on behalf of both animals and plants.

> What is the message signaled by the hordes of diatoms, flashing their microscopic lights in the night sea? What truth is expressed by the legions of the barnacles, whitening the rocks with their habitations, each small creature within finding the necessities of its existence in the sweep of the surf? And what is the meaning of so tiny a being as the transparent wisp of protoplasm that is a sea lace, existing for some reason inscrutable to us—a reason that demands its presence by the trillion amid the rocks and weeds of the shore? The meaning haunts and ever eludes us, and in its very pursuit we approach the ultimate mystery of Life itself.
> —Rachel Carson

Green Spot

Time Required	3, 30 minutes periods over at least 24 hours
Group Size	Any
Materials	Drawing materials
Location	The wilder the better
Indoor Use	No
Intended Result	Establishment of a special relationship with one spot; appreciation of the natural world

SUMMARY: Students get to know one spot well by returning to it several times over the course of a 24 hour period or longer. Each will be alone for at least half an hour for each visit. The student will become familiar with her green place under different conditions of light, heat, humidity, and activity.

The student should be willing to sit quietly, preferably in an area rich with plant life. She might think of herself as a plant and emulate the qualities that she sees around her.

> The earth never tires;
> The earth is rude, silent, incomprehensible at first—
>   Nature is rude and incomprehensible at first;
> Be not discouraged—keep on—there are divine things,
>   well envelop'd;
> I swear to you there are divine things more beautiful
>   than words can tell.
>   —Walt Whitman
>
>
>
> In the hope of reaching the moon men fail to see the flowers that blossom at their feet.
>   —Albert Schweitzer

PROCEDURE: Each person chooses a spot that feels good to her; she should be out of sight of other humans, yet close enough to hear the signal to return. Everyone remains quiet and still at each spot. Here are some things each person can think about while there:
—What do you see around you in the big picture? Close by?

—What sounds do you hear? Draw a map of the sounds and from what directions they come.
—What attracts you to that place?
—What was this place like 10 years ago? 100? 1000? What might it be like 10, or 100, or 1000 years from now?
—What plants do you see? What animals or signs of animals do you see?
—How much do the plants around you move? What sounds do they make? How many shades of green do you see? How many different kinds of plants? What would it be like to be one of these plants?

Be sure each person knows how to get back to the exact same spot. Each returns to the group when she hears the signal (perhaps a hoot, or a whistle blast).

The return can be at different times during the day, when there has been a change in weather, at night, at dusk or dawn.

FOLLOW-UP: Encourage students to find a green place near their homes, a single special spot which they can visit in different weathers and seasons.

Being With Trees

Time Required	30 minutes or longer
Group size	Any
Materials	Blindfolds, art supplies, yardsticks, field guide
Location	Among the trees
Indoor Use	No
Intended Result	Enhanced appreciation of, kinship with, and love for trees

SUMMARY: Students get to know trees via various sensory activities.

PROCEDURE:

ACTIVITY #1: In *Sharing Nature with Children*, Joseph Cornell offers a blindfold activity entitled "Meet a Tree." A blindfolded person has a partner who leads her to a tree and encourages her to get to know it with specific questions and statements. Examples: "Is this tree still alive? Can you put your arms around it? Is the tree older than you are?" Then the blindfolded person is led back to a starting point by an indirect route and challenged to find her tree with the blindfold removed. "Suddenly," Cornell says, "as they search for the tree, what was a forest becomes a collection of very individual trees."

ACTIVITY #2: Blindfold all (or a large segment) of your students. Lead them into an area with different types of trees. Let them feel the bark of different species, and come up with a group name for each. Then lead them back out and let them find their trees with blindfolds removed.

ACTIVITY #3: Choose a tree. Measure its height. The best way to do this is to measure the tree's shadow, then have someone measure your shadow. Your Height (YH) divided by Your Shadow's height (YS) = the Tree's Height (TH) divided by the Tree's Shadow's (TS) height. Multiply your height times the tree's shadow's height and divide by your shadow's height to get the tree's height. OR:

$$\frac{YH \times TS}{YS} = TH$$

If sunlight is not available because of shade or clouds, have someone stand next to the tree. Go to a point 60 feet away where you can see the tree and the person clearly. Use a pencil or stick and measure how many of the person's heights will fit in the height of the tree. Multiply that number by the person's approximate height; you now have the tree's approximate height.

A forest is a perfect example of the law of return in action. Trees give back to the earth more than they take, while building up humus, and enriching the soil by the minerals that have been carried up to the leaves in the rising sap. By nature man is a forest dweller. He was cradled in the tropics. His food was the fruit of trees. He possessed the secret of adaptation to his environment, so that health, gentleness, beauty and strength were enjoyed to the full. In his forest setting man was conscious of his relationship to God and of his unity with all living things.
— Richard St. Barbe Baker

The following activities occur after each student chooses a special tree of her own:

ACTIVITY #4: Draw the outline (silhouette) of your tree. Does it have an unusual skeletal structure that is shared with others of its species?

ACTIVITY #5: Draw a map of the tree's home place (about 20 feet in each direction). Make it a bird's eye view, and map the nearby trees, rocks, etc. Do you see your tree's parent tree? Any probable children of your tree?

ACTIVITY #6: Draw a to-scale pattern of the tree's bark. Draw a bud. Make a detailed drawing of a leaf. Or simply do a rubbing of your tree's bark (by putting paper against the tree and coloring with a pencil.) Compare with rubbings of other barks. Smell your tree. Put your nose up to the bark. Smell one of its leaves. What does it smell like?

What makes its home in your tree? Are there nests? Insects? Does it serve as shelter, cover, or food source to other plants or animals?

Touch the tree. Feel its bark and describe the texture. How old is the tree? Does the tree feel old or young? What kind of life has it had?

ACTIVITY #7: Write a letter to your tree. What do you want to tell it? Return to the group and share with others your special tree.

Go back and read your letter to the tree out loud. Stay for a while and listen for a response. Do you hear any? Some people do and some don't. If the tree communicates something you can write down, then write it. (In a recent interview with Malidoma Patrice Some, D. Patrick Miller said, "When I sit beneath a tree and get some kind of feeling or message, the problem is that it's not verbal. I am always struggling to use words to figure out what it means." Malidoma responds: "When the message resists being put into words, it is very important to respect that. There are many realities that die the moment they are wrapped in words... That realm is asking you to recognize it by respecting its wordlessness. Sooner or later, you'll realize that your experience by the tree constitutes an entirely different type of communication.")

ACTIVITY #8: Divide into groups whose trees are close to one another. Create skits of what your trees have seen or experienced in their lifetimes.

O dreamy, gloomy friendly trees,
I came along your narrow track
To bring my gifts unto your knees
And gifts did you give back;
For when I brought this heart that burns—
These thoughts that bitterly repine—
And laid them here among the ferns
And the hum of boughs divine,
Ye, vastest breathers of the air,
Shook down with slow and mighty poise
Your coolness on the human care,
Your wonder on its toys,
Your greenness on the heart's despair,
Your darkness on its noise.
                    —Herbert Trench

A Fallen Giant

Time Required	10 minutes or longer
Group Size	Any
Materials	Optional: hand lenses
Location	On the trail
Indoor Use	No
Intended Result	Understanding the life cycle of a tree and its connection to other beings

SUMMARY: Students explore a large fallen tree for signs of other life.

PROCEDURE: While walking on the trail, look for a large fallen tree in a decomposing state. Ask the students what it is that they see. The obvious answer is: a dead tree. You can explain the paradoxes in nature, where when a living entity dies, it then becomes the source of life for many others.

This tree was once a seed. It was nourished by sun, water, and soil nutrients to become this tree. It was shade for others, produced oxygen and water, disposed of carbon dioxide, and helped make this a more livable world.

Now it has stopped living and has become a source of life for others. Termites use it for food. Spiders set their snares beside it. Moss calls it home along with some mushrooms. Birds peck at bark and eat the insects. As this happens, the tree slowly breaks down into soil, starting the cycle of life over again. Study the tree and its different aspects of decomposition. Look at it through hand lenses. Talk about what you see.

FOLLOW-UP: What other entities die and give life again by decomposing in a natural cycle? How long ago did this tree die? Why does it take different trees different amounts of time to decay? What would happen in the forest if all dead trees were removed and not allowed to decompose? How would it affect soil, insects, birds, mammals, and the future of the forest?

> While the terms 'high quality timber' and 'low quality timber' are frequently used in timber management, nature does not assign such values to trees. In the natural community, there is always a productive use for a tree, living as well as dead, whether as a wildlife nesting place, food source, windbreak, soil stabilizer, or eventual component of soil. (Alabama Environmental Council, 1994)

BACKGROUND: Clearcutting.

Clearcutting, sometimes called even-age logging, is the method of cutting down all trees in a given area within a short period of time. In selective cutting, or selection management, individual trees or small groups of trees in a healthy natural forest are chosen for cutting and the rest of the forest is left alive.

U.S. National Forests did not even allow clearcutting before 1976. Now in our national forests the trees are cut, then the site is scraped by bulldozers. The vegetation, debris, and small animals are pushed into piles and burned. Save America's Forests contends that this destroys the genetic blueprint of the site.

According to the Western North Carolina Alliance, "Soil temperatures in recent clearcuts can exceed 140 degrees, very harmful to shade- and moisture-loving forest organisms...Recent research on salamanders has indicated that United States Forest Service clearcutting may be killing upwards of 14 million a year."

Clearing and burning the land is often followed by the application of herbicides so that unwanted vegetation will not interfere with the planting of single species stands of timber. In Western North Carolina, home to around 150 species of trees, only 10 are considered commercially desirable. The rest are considered, and called, "junk trees;" they are destroyed.

Save America's Forests argues that, "Natural forests are filled with many types of trees, plants, animals, and healthy abundant soil...The natural forest is filled with old, middle age and young trees, and is naturally resistant to damage from fire, floods and drought. In contrast, these artificial stands of trees are...by design meant to be devoid of all of the magnificent, diverse, and myriad forms of plant and animal life which have made up the fabric of life in America's forests for thousands of years."

Some people argue that clearcutting is good because it maintains different stages of forest succession across the landscape; after all, people have interrupted the <u>natural</u> disturbances of fire and infestation that have historically maintained forest succession. The ecocentric perspective has a number of counterarguments. For example, clearcutting takes place more frequently than natural disturbances; the planting of relatively few species can't replicate natural ecosystems. Most importantly, the ecocentric point of view reflects Commoner's Third Law of Ecology: "Nature Knows Best." We don't know enough about natural disturbance patterns to try to replicate them through cutting. We don't understand all of a mature forest's structural characteristics. According to the Alabama Environmental Council's *Landowners Don't Miss Out*, clearcutting does make occasional sense, such as where the goal is to return the land to natural succession and one cutting is part of the plan. But as a general policy, clearcutting may be a disaster.

Albert Meier and David Cameron Duffy of the University of Georgia studied the effects of clearcutting on forests cut 87 years ago. They found that the sites are not returning to their original condition, lacking the ground cover of wildflowers and other plants that were part of the original forest's ecosystem. According to Paul Raeburn of the Associated Press, Harvard University's Glenn Matlock said Meier's work was "an incredible study" that illustrates "the concept that a forest is more than trees—it's a complex community." Meier studied the cove forests or hollows of the southern Appalachians. Less than 1 per cent of the old growth cove forest is left, but the U.S. Forest Service continues to allow cutting of old growth timber. (Sources: Associated Press, *Bankhead Monitor*, October, 1992)

The Forest Service should be encouraged to err on the side of conservation and reduce significantly or eliminate clearcutting. Since only 5% of our original native forests are left, it is especially important that we preserve and protect them from clearcutting. This 5% contains especially great potential: potential for science and medicine, potential for life in its genetic diversity, potential for people who need the wildness and complexity of a natural forest.

Discovering Plants

Time Required	60 minutes or longer
Group Size	Individuals or small groups
Materials	None
Location	Outdoors
Indoor Use	Yes
Intended Result	Increased appreciation of plants

SUMMARY: Students compare different plants to get an idea of their diversity while focusing on the nature of plants and their qualities.

PROCEDURE: Each student or small group finds three different plants growing near one another. Do not disturb the plants. The students can draw the plants and then attempt to answer the following questions.
—How are the three plants similar? Different?
—What is different about leaf and vein patterns?
—How do these plants reproduce?
—What does each need to survive?
—What defines a plant?
—What are common links between all plants?
—Does anything depend on these plants for food? Shelter? Cover?
—Do these plants have any medicinal uses?
—What might happen if these plants becomes extinct?
—What might these plants be used for?

FOLLOW-UP: How is a plant different from an animal? One dictionary definition for plants: "living thing without sense organs that cannot move about." One for animals: "a being capable of feeling and voluntary motion." Do you agree with the definitions? If not, how would you change them?

Plants can be useful to humans in many different ways. They collectively have many different characteristics. They are a very renewable resource. Think creatively about how plants might be substituted for the following:
—nylon rope (rope can be made of grasses, yucca fiber, poplar bark fiber)
—backpack (grass or oak split basket)
—sleeping bag (leaves, milkweed seed pods fluffed up, and a debris survival hut all help insulate)
—lighter (bow drill to start fire)
How about: knife, pen, camera, cup, plate, spoon, cooking pot, refrigerator, plastic bag, chair.

Flower in the crannied wall,
I pluck you out of the crannies,
I hold you here, root and all, in my hand,
Little flower—but if I could understand
What you are, root and all, and all in all,
I should know what God and man is.
—Alfred, Lord Tennyson

Background: Forest Food

by Mike "Snake" Offutt, *Bankhead Monitor*. Used with permission.

"The wild edibles, where are they?" That is the question you may ask if you go out and seek them. In most areas the majority of them are gone. Gone are the giant nut trees and their delicious mast crops. Gone are the mature fruit bearers. Gone are the succulent berries, herbs, and root plants. Gone where? The nut and fruit producers have fallen to the saw. The more tender plants have been crushed and broken as their tall neighbors were felled upon them. The ones that survived the traction and weight of the wheels of trucks and skidders, the abrasion of cables and dragging logs, did not survive the perils brought on by unfiltered, direct sunlight and soil erosion. Good luck if you go looking for much to eat in a twenty to thirty year old pine forest, which is a latent product of a clear cut. With most of the topsoil gone, the subsoils and clays have become highly acidic from the layers of pine straw that cover the ground. Pine trees, scattered patches of honeysuckle vines, poison ivy, briars, and not much else is what you find in this environment If you go walking through one of these areas, you may wonder what the animals eat. Maybe that has something to do with the fact that you haven't seen many, if any, animals during your visit.

Transition Zones and Micro-Environments

Time Required	60 minutes or longer
Group Size	Any
Materials	Cards
Location	Outdoors
Indoor Use	No
Intended Result	Knowledge of the complexity and diversity of transition zones

SUMMARY: Students visit and learn about transition zones.

PREPARATION: Thorough knowledge of the area through which you are traveling.

PROCEDURE: Communicate about the micro-environments and transition zones in the area where your group is located. If, for example, the group is exploring a forest environment, the following clues will tell them when they've moved into a different forest micro-environment:

WATER—"riparian zones" are areas around streams, rivers, wetlands

TEMPERATURE—differs with wind patterns, amount of sunlight, ridge or valley

LIGHT—meadow versus deep forest

GEOGRAPHY—valley versus ridge top, flat lands, cliffs, etc.

VEGETATION—how is it different from the way it was in other areas you hiked through?

HUMAN CONSTRUCTED FEATURES—fencerows, roads, power lines, clearcuts, etc.

NATURAL EVENTS—fire scars, ice storm damage, etc.

"Transition Zones," also called "Ecotones," are places where different forest types or environments meet—the edge of a field or beside a stream, for example. Transition zones often offer greater diversity of species and are usually the best places to observe wildlife.

As you travel through the forest, learn to read the woods. Open your senses, observe, compare, contrast, think, analyze, appreciate. The following activity will help.

Participants will locate and choose a transition zone with easy to observe differences, such as a field near a stream with woods nearby, perhaps with a path going through the area. Then they will:
1. Pace off an area about 300 yards on a side.
2. Divide into three small groups.
3. Have each group draw a map of the area. Partition the map so that each group is assigned a different micro-environment to study. For example, one would examine the field, one the riparian zone, and one the woods.
4. Do an inventory of plants. What are the common species in your area? How many different plant species can you locate?
5. Write a general physical description of your zone: soil type, temperature, light, cover (amount of trees, shrubs, etc.), food sources available for animals, availability of water.
6. Report back to the group after 30-60 minutes and compare results. Discuss the past history of the area. Have humans impacted this area? If so, what signs do you see (old fence line, house site, piles of rocks, orchard, signs of logging, etc.)?

If possible, do this activity in more than one location and compare findings.

John Muir wrote: "We are now on what may be called the second plateau of the Range, after making many small ups and downs over belts of hill-waves, with, of course, corresponding changes in the vegetation." The key words here are "of course." Of course the vegetation changes with changes in climate and altitude. Even a difference of a few hundred feet can mean a major shift in ecosystems. And yet how aware are most people of something that to John Muir is simply a matter "of course?" The forests of the North Carolina mountains, for example, are 98% different at the summits than at the lower levels. Subtle changes contribute to the wealth and variety of life; life has found ways to adjust and thrive throughout a large range of these small changes. Of course!

Tic Tac Trail

Time Required	15 minutes or longer
Group Size	Any
Materials	Cards
Location	Outdoors
Indoor Use	Yes (variation)
Intended Result	Enjoyment, increased knowledge, teamwork

SUMMARY: Bingo cards with natural objects on them are created and used.

PREPARATION: Bingo cards can be made to any level of difficulty. With children just beginning to read, the cards can use pictures instead of words. With botany or zoology students the names of species can be put on the cards. A sample card for 7 year olds:

- oak tree
- mammal
- red leaf
- spider web
- smooth rock
- berry
- rotting leaf
- insect
- poison ivy

A sample card for 12 year olds:

- butterfly
- bone
- tree habitat
- bird nest
- feather
- animal track
- quartz
- toadstool
- acorn

A sample card for 17 year olds:

- woodpecker hole
- herbivore
- sign of lightning
- snakeskin
- animal burrow
- wildflower(specific)
- animal scat
- mint
- fungus

PROCEDURE: Students will attempt to find the items on the cards, either filling the card or finding a horizontal, vertical, or diagonal line as in Tic Tac Toe. Students can work alone or in teams. Each "find" must have verification from another student. If several rounds are played, students could take turns being "verifiers" or referees.

Visual ideas include: ant, beaver, black birch tree, dam, bee, dogwood flower, erosion, fat wood (firestarter), five-needled pine, lichen, moss, Northern Red Oak, raccoon track, rhododendron, snake, spring, twist tie or other trash, turkey vulture, wasp, white pine cone, woodpecker hole, woodpecker.

A card might also involve other senses, including sound (woodpecker sound, squirrel chatter, babbling brook), smell (pine heartwood, flower, skunkweed), or touch (rough, smooth, oily).

VARIATIONS:

1. With a small group in a van or car, van bingo can be played en route to a nature activity and can include various natural and human artifacts that can be seen from the van and that help establish a sense of place. Students on each seat share a card.

2. Classroom: While outdoors with real animals and plants is preferred, the group can play Tic Tac Trail in the classroom. Pictures of natural objects can be drawn or gathered from books and magazines. These will be used as the basis for making the bingo cards. The "caller" holds up the picture and the students try to find those objects on their bingo cards without identifying them aloud.

Camouflage

Time Required	15 minutes or longe
Group Size	Minimum of 8
Materials	None
Location	The wilder the better
Indoor Use	Yes (variations)
Intended Result	Knowledge of the importance of camouflage and its variety of forms

SUMMARY: Students play variations on hide-and-seek to learn about camouflage.

BACKGROUND: Many animals have or use camouflage that is crucial to their survival. Camouflage allows them not to be seen by their predators or their prey. Color, texture, body shape, markings, lighting, season, and time of day all are factors in camouflage. The ability to remain motionless and the ability to hide behind or build a disguise from surrounding materials are important camouflage techniques.

PROCEDURE: This is hide and seek with a twist. One student (the seeker) stands in the center of the designated area, closes her eyes, and counts to 25 (or 10, or 50) out loud. Everyone else runs as far as they can in any direction and hides wherever they can as long as they are within view of the seeker. The seeker calls out the name or position of anyone she can see. A person who is seen is out. The seeker closes her eyes and counts to 10. Those still hiding move closer and hide in that time.

The cycle is repeated until everyone is found. The last person to be seen is the seeker in the next round.

VARIATIONS:
1. Play the game at night with a single flashlight or lantern. The animals creep in to see how close they can get. The major challenge at night is silent movement.
2. Choose an area along the trail. Divide the crew into two groups. Send half ahead and ask them to camouflage themselves within 20 feet of the trail. They might hide behing a tree, crouch behing a bush, lie flat in a hollow, use leaves or dead branches as cover. The other half walks down the trail and tries to find as many people as possible. Then the two groups change places. Remind the students to respect the plant and animal life of the area where they will hide.
3. Have students choose a spot along a trail that would provide good cam-

ouflage for an animal. Have them draw, color, cut out, and place a picture of the animal in the spot. The spot should be within five feet of the trail. Students walk slowly down the trail and try to spot one another's drawings. Make sure that each artist knows where her picture is so that all can be taken with you when you leave.

4. Classroom: Teach students about camouflage. Have them draw pictures of animals camouflaged in their natural environments.
5. Classroom: Dye small macaroni noodles with two different food colors, red and green. Scatter them randomly in the school yard grass so that the green noodles are camouflaged. Have students hunt for the "macaroni beasts." They'll find more red than green, and the shorter the search time, the larger percentage of red to green they'll find.

FOLLOW-UP:
1. Whenever possible, show students examples of camouflage in nature. This includes walking sticks, insects that mimic leaves or bark (especially moths), the speckled appearance of baby birds. Insects are excellent examples and can best be seen mid-day on hot sunny days when they're active.
2. Share these viewing tips:

Being aware of animal camouflage can help if you want to see animals in the wild. You must be especially attentive. You must also be willing to camouflage yourself. Don't wear bright colors. The smaller the group you travel in the better.

Quietness, stillness, and patience will offer an opportunity to see more. Students on Outward Bound courses often ask why they don't see large animals on the trail. While the numbers of large animals in U.S. forests has declined significantly through the years, a major reason these animals aren't seen is the amount of noise generated by a group of campers. Other viewing tips include:

— Be a good guest. You are only visiting. Allow animals to stay in a natural state. Small animals are easily stressed by humans handling them—many can become dangerously defensive. If you have a compelling reason to pick up or touch an animal, do so with care and sensitivity.
— Look for edges: stream meets bank, sky meets land, forest meets field, ridge meets hillside. Animals are more active in these transitional zones. Look during the "edges" of the day, dawn and sunset, because animals are more active then.
— Look for more than the animal itself: hair, scat, skin (snake), tracks and trails, gnawings, sounds, voices and movements, homes (nests, holes, dens), smells (bear, skunk).

Sheet Shake

Time Required	20 minutes
Group Size	Any
Materials	White sheet or garbage bag, magnifiers
Location	Outdoors
Indoor Use	No
Intended Result	Better understanding of camouflage, habitat, the diversity of insect life

SUMMARY: Students learn about insects, their variety, and how they hide by studying the insects in a bush.

PROCEDURE: Place the sheet or pillowcase under a shrub or bush. Shake the branches vigorously and watch what falls onto the sheet. Note: students should not be under the bush or shrub while it is being shaken. Sunlight shining directly on the sheet with no shadows makes it easier to see. Things to observe:
1. How many legs are on each bug? Find six-legged's and eight-legged's. Notice if there are wings; if so, how many pairs. Note the body structure: head, thorax, abdomen. An insect has three body parts and six legs. A spider has two body parts and eight legs.
2. Look closely at the head and jaws. Is it a meat or a plant eater? What might eat it?
3. Can you find more than one stage of insect life—egg, larva, adult?
4. Why has each creature chosen to live here?

FOLLOW-UP: Remind the students that this bush or shrub is the insects' habitat—their home. Shake the sheet gently over the "home" bush to allow them to return. Teach students the importance of handling bugs—if the bugs must be handled at all—very gently.

"Sheet Shake" is adapted from "A Teacher's Guide to Environmental Education," by The Alabama Environmental Council. Used with permission.

Doin' The Eatin' Thang

Time Required	15 minutes per round, 4-5 rounds
Group Size	8-15
Materials	Blindfolds
Location	Open area
Indoor Use	Yes
Intended Result	Understanding of how predator and prey try to survive in the wild

SUMMARY: Students stalk one another in a game of blindfold tag to learn about predators and prey.

> Most of us walk unseeing through the world, unaware alike of its beauties, its wonders, and the strange and sometimes terrible intensity of the lives that are being lived about us. So it is that the activities of the insect predators and parasites are known to few. Perhaps we may have noticed an oddly shaped insect of ferocious mien on a bush in the garden and been dimly aware that the praying mantis lives at the expense of other insects. But we see with understanding eye only if we have walked in the garden at night and here and there with a flashlight have glimpsed the mantis stealthily creeping upon her prey. Then we sense something of the drama of the hunter and the hunted. Then we begin to feel something of that relentlessly pressing force by which nature controls her own.
> —Rachel Carson

PREPARATION: Familiarize yourself with specific predator/prey relationships.

PROCEDURE: Relate to students the relationship of predator and prey. All students are blindfolded and mixed in an open area within a large circle. Each student stalks the other students, catching them with two-handed tag, while avoiding being caught. No running is allowed. If someone begins to leave the circle, instructors touch his or her shoulder and turn them toward the center of the circle. Anyone who has fallen 'prey' removes his or her blindfold and backs out of the circle repeating "I'm out, I'm out." Those "out" help turn those still in the game back toward the center of the circle.

Students devise their own methods of stalking and escaping. The winner is the last one to have escaped predation.

FOLLOW-UP: What defenses did you use? What defenses do animals have to avoid becoming prey (porcupines, skunks, bobcats, frogs, specific insects, etc.)? As a predator, how did you find your prey.

VARIATION: Shark and tuna can be played with a smaller group or area. Two players are blindfolded and given a whistle. One is predator, the other prey. The predator calls, the prey answers. The rest of the group keeps the two safely within the circle.

> The fact that in nature one creature may cause pain to another and even deal with it instinctively in the most cruel way, is a harsh mystery that weighs on us as long as we live.
> —Albert Schweitzer

Animal Line-up

Time Required	10-15 minutes
Group Size	8-15
Materials	None
Location	Any
Indoor Use	Yes
Intended Result	Successful problem-solving and teamwork

SUMMARY: Students depict animals, but only they know for certain which animal they are. They arrange themselves in order using animal sounds or motions only.

PROCEDURE:
1. Assign each student an animal which makes a distinctive noise. Have them line themselves up according to the size of the animal they portray, smallest to largest, or according to population on the planet, least to greatest. No talking allowed.
2. Mix animals that make a sound with animals that don't and have students line themselves up again. The animals which make no sound will have to figure out how to communicate what they are.

VARIATIONS:
1. Let the students pick their own animals so that the instructor doesn't know what they are either.
2. Take sound out altogether and have the students identify themselves to each other through gestures, then line up as in #1.

ANIMAL EXAMPLES: Bee, Chihuahua, Cow, Crow, Elephant, Great Dane, Grizzly Bear, Cardinal, Monkey, Mosquito, Mountain Lion, Mouse, Pig, Rooster, Cicada, Sheep, Turkey.

I'd sooner exchange ideas with the birds on earth than learn to carry on intergalactic communications with some obscure race of humanoids on a satellite planet from the world of Betelgeuse. First things first.

—Edward Abbey

Speak For The Animals

Time Required	1 hour
Group Size	8 or more
Materials	None
Location	Anywhere
Indoor Use	Yes
Intended Result	Compassion for and empathy with our fellow creatures

SUMMARY: Each person thinks of an animal and becomes its voice by writing about it.

PROCEDURE: Have each person think of an animal that has characteristics the person would like to have. Have the group spread out so that each person has a quiet spot. Each thinks about her animal. What characteristics does the animal have that the person admires or would like to have? What is the animal's life like?

Write a story about an event in the life of the animal. Tell it either from the animal's or from an outsider's point of view.

Write from the animal's point of view about changes it would like to make in its environment.

FOLLOW-UP: Everyone brings her animal voice, in story or in person, back to the circle to share with everyone else.

Going Further — This is one example of the type of project creative teachers and parents can do with children.

Mary Moten's 5th Grade Class at EPIC Elementary School in Birmingham, Alabama decided to draw a mural of Alabama's Threatened and Endangered Species. Each student researched one of the 60 species; they wrote about their animals, learned to draw them, then created the mural. Ms. Moten wrote a play, and the children represented their animals; their parents helped create costumes. Parents found a local company to donate 10,000 printed copies of the mural and an accompanying guide book — profits from sales of the poster go into an endangered species fund. Before they were through, the students had visited their state's governor, spoken to both houses of the legislature, and given other public performances, all in the costumes of their adopted species.

For more details about Ms. Moten's project, write Endangered Species, P.O. Box 55341, Birmingham, AL 35255.

We are the generation that searched on Mars for evidence of life but couldn't rouse enough moral sense to stop the destruction of even the grandest manifestations of life on earth. In that sense we are like the Romans whose works of art, architecture and engineering inspire our awe but whose traffic in slaves and gladiatorial combat is mystifying and loathsome.

—Dr. Roger Payne, whale conservationist

Humanity has four and a half billion passionate advocates—but how many speak for the polar bear? for the manatee? for the crocodile? for the gray wolf? for the Bengal tiger? for the Mexican grizzly? for the iguana? for the beaded lizard? for the sperm whale? for the caiman? for the monitor? for the kangaroo? for the ring-tailed cat? for the desert tortoise? for the moose? for the native trout? for the humpback whale? for the dolphin? for the wallaby? for the koala bear? for the panda? for the caribou? for the red wolf? for the panther? for the musk-ox? for the black leopard? for the snow leopard? for the wild yak? for the mustang? for the Dall sheep? for the alligator? for the hippopotamus? for the pupfish? for the snail darter? for the harp seal? for all of the world's endangered?

It is a man's duty to speak for the voiceless. A woman's obligation to aid the defenseless. Human needs do not take precedence over other forms of life; we must share this lovely, delicate, vapor-clouded little planet with all.

—Edward Abbey

Folding Poem

Time Required	30 minutes
Group Size	8 or more
Materials	Paper and pen
Location	Anywhere
Indoor Use	Yes
Intended Result	Teamwork and enjoyment, sharing, appreciation of points-of-view

SUMMARY: Participants write a poem together with only partial knowledge of what else has been written.

PROCEDURE: The first person writes a line of a poem about the living world and passes it to the second person. She writes a line that rhymes with the first person's line, then writes another; she folds the poem so that the next person sees only the last line. The poem proceeds around the circle with each participant rhyming with the line above, adding a line of her own, and folding the paper so that only the last line is visible. When the poem gets back to the first person, she writes the final line.

NOTE: This works best in an outdoor setting, especially when the group has just shared an experience or a special sighting of a plant or animal.

EarthNotes: The Living World

"There are more insects in one square mile of rural land than human beings on the entire earth." (Cousteau, 1981)

"Ethiopia's forest cover has declined from 30% of its land to 1% of its land in 40 years. India's forest cover has declined from more than 50% to around 14% since 1900. In Brazil, where Chico Mendes died protecting what he called the 'lungs of the planet,' 20 million acres are being cut annually. In the tropics, only one tree is being planted for every 10 cut." (Stead & Stead, 1992)

"Biological diversity—the variety among living organisms and the ecological communities they inhabit—is more threatened now than at any time in the past 65 million years. Tropical deforestation is the main force behind the crisis, but the destruction of wetlands, coral reefs, and temperate forests also plays an important role." (World Resources Institute, 1992)

"The diversity of species is necessary for the normal functioning of ecosystems and the biosphere as a whole. The genetic material in wild species contributes billions of dollars yearly to the world economy in the form of improved crop species, new drugs and medicines, and raw materials for industry. But utility aside, there are also moral, ethical, cultural, aesthetic, and purely scientific reasons for conserving wild beings." (The Brundtland Report, 1987)

"Of the 4 million to 30 million species currently inhabiting the planet, some scientists predict that 100 species a day will be driven to extinction in the next 30 years because of economic growth activities. Most of the extinction is occurring in the tropics, home to between 50% and 80% of these species. Extinction is nothing new; 99% of the species that have inhabited the Earth are now extinct. However, the current rate is 1,000 times higher than that of any other period in history." (Stead & Stead, 1990)

"The shrimp industry alone discards about nine pounds of young fish for every pound of shrimp harvested. Among the discarded fish are a number that would have high commercial value at maturity." (Council on Environmental Quality, 1992)

"There is still time to save species and their ecosystems. It is an indispensable prerequisite for sustainable development. Our failure to do so will not be forgiven by future generations." (The Brundtland Report, 1987)

Readings: The Living World

What prizes the town and the tower?
Only what the pine-tree yields.
      —Ralph Waldo Emerson

We may imagine a time when, in the infancy of the human race, some enterprising mortal crept into a hollow in a rock for shelter. Every child begins the world again, to some extent, and loves to stay out doors, even in wet and cold...From the cave we have advanced to roofs of palm leaves, of bark and boughs, of linen woven and stretched, of grass and straw, of boards and shingles, of stones and tiles. At last, we know not what it is to live in the open air, and our lives are domestic in more senses than we think... It would be well perhaps if we were to spend more of our days and nights without any obstruction between us and the celestial bodies, if the poet did not speak so much from under a roof, or the saint dwell there so long. Birds do not sing in caves, nor do doves cherish their innocence in dovecots.
      —Henry David Thoreau

There are woods that are plain to look at, but not to look into.
      —Aldo Leopold

If we see any immediate utility in a plant we foster it. If for any reason we find its presence undesirable or merely a matter of indifference, we may condemn it to destruction forthwith. Besides the various plants that are poisonous to man or his livestock, or crowd out food plants, many are marked for destruction merely because, according to our narrow view, they happen to be in the wrong place at the wrong time. Many others are destroyed merely because they happen to be associates of the unwanted plants.

The earth's vegetation is part of a web of life in which there are intimate and essential relations between plants and the earth, between plants and other plants, between plants and animals. Sometimes we have no choice but to disturb these relationships, but we should do so thoughtfully, with full awareness that what we do may have consequences remote both in time and place.
      —Rachel Carson

Breathe your pure carbon dioxide to a leaf and sense it breathing fresh oxygen back to you.
      —John Seed and Joanna Macy

Hast thou named all the birds without a gun?
Loved the wood-rose and left it on its stalk?
O, be my friend, and teach me to be thine.
      —Ralph Waldo Emerson

I lay among the ferns,
Where they lifted their fronds innumerable, in the greenwood wilderness,
    like wings winnowing the air;
And their voices went past me continually.

And I listened, and lo! softly inaudibly raining I heard not the voices of the
    ferns only, but of all living creatures;
Voices of mountain and star,
Of cloud and forest and ocean,
And of the little rills tumbling amid the rocks,
And of the high tops where the moss-beds are and the springs arise.
As the wind at mid-day rains whitening over the grass,
As the night-bird glimmers a moment, fleeting between the lonely watcher
    and the moon,
So softly inaudibly they rained
Where I sat silent...

Who should understand the words of the ferns lifting their fronds innumer-
    able?
What man shall go forth into the world, holding his life in his open palm —
With high adventurous joy from sunrise to sunset —
Fearless, in his sleeve laughing, having outflanked his enemies?
His heart like Nature's garden — that all men abide in —
Free, where the great winds blow, rains fall, and the sun shines,
And manifold growths come forth and scatter their fragrance —
They who sit by the road and are weary shall rise up
As he passes. They who despair shall arise.
      —Edward Carpenter

Notes:

GLOBAL AND LOCAL

Global And Local...

Being out in the wilderness without the comforts of home for so long has given me more respect for nature and has taught me how unimportant most material goods really are. I don't need much to be happy, as long as I am dry and warm and keeping a positive attitude, life can be as fulfilling as I want and care to make it.
—Outward Bound student, age 18

I feel that the instructors and this course and the crew have all given me the most important gift of my life, the gift of seeing the Earth through Nature's eyes and living on the Earth through Nature's ways. I am thankful for Outward Bound for teaching me to walk on the Earth and not above it.
—Outward Bound student, age 16

We all need more connections between ourselves and the natural world. We tend to **think** locally without seeing that we **act** globally. As we learn to walk "on the Earth and not above it," we can see more clearly what effect our lifestyles have on the rest of the living world. We will always be consumers of resources, but we can choose to consume less, and we can choose

John Heine

actions that support and build the natural wealth of the planet. This section focuses on some of the issues about which we should think globally and on some ways we can think and act locally to make things better.

The human population of the planet continues to increase and now stands at about 5 1/2 billion. The opinions given throughout this section on how many people the world can sustain are dramatic and sobering. We do know that if each of us made careful choices about how we consume and what we do with our waste that we would relieve much of the immediate pressure on our environment. For example, "Each year [in the United States], some 350 million gallons of motor oil are improperly disposed of by do-it-yourselfers, the rough equivalent of three Exxon Valdez oil spills every month." (Makower, 1992)

We should work to stop the major sources of industrial pollution, and at the same time we should work to change our personal consumption habits. We should try to preserve old growth forests throughout the world, and at the same time we should seek out recycled paper and purchase local produce. While we work for clean rivers and estuaries, we should conserve water in our own homes. While we take a stand on global clean air issues, we should make intelligent decisions about our personal driving habits and needs. We need to think about the Global, the Local, and the Personal, because our choices now will affect the range of choices available to our children and their children and all the children to come.

In *Time Wars*, Jeremy Rifkin quotes an Iroquois chief to show the unique and exemplary method the Iroquois used in making decisions: **"We are looking ahead, as is one of the first mandates given to us as chiefs, to make sure [that] every decision we make relates to the welfare and well-being of the seventh generation to come, and that is the basis by which we make decisions in council. We consider: Will this be to the benefit of the seventh generation: This is a guideline."**

World Dinner

Time Required	Food preparation plus 30 minutes
Group Size	10 or more
Materials	Map, food
Location	Outdoors
Indoor Use	Yes
Intended Result	The ability to think globally (and locally) about food

SUMMARY: A meal of beans and rice is prepared and distributed to representatives of various countries proportional to the average food intake of that country's citizens.

PREPARATION: Read the background information at the end of the activity. Prepare a meal of rice and beans. Write the names of the countries on the graph below on separate sheets of paper. The number of names used can be varied depending on number of participants.

PROCEDURE: Students choose a country from a hat. Students guess the average caloric intake per day of their country. Using the key below, the instructor will distribute food as follows:

COUNTRY	CALORIES PER DAY	SPOONFUL EQUIVALENT
Mozambique	1793	1
Low Income Countries	2100	1+
China	2620	1 1/2
Middle Income Countries	2719	1 1/2
Industrial Countries	3357	2-
U.S.	3682	2+
Germany	3769	2+

Students should be encouraged to remedy the inequality of food distribution in their group.

VARIATIONS:
1. Food is much more effective than non-food items such as marbles or dried beans for communicating the message about food deprivation. Candy such as jelly beans can also be used. Divide the group into industrialized and low-income and give the industrialized citizens twice as many plus one small candies. Rather than have the group try to remedy the candy inequality, let the have-nots experience it; on another day, reverse the roles.

2. Say you are going to distribute the supper equally, with half of the group getting beans and rice, the other half getting meat. Beef jerky is a simple-to-carry meat product. What you will be distributing, however, is the caloric equivalency of the meat and non-meat meals. It takes 16-18 non-meat calories to produce one calorie of grain fed beef. Two cups (16 ounces) of beans and rice = approximately 400 calories. The meat-eaters will receive 22-25 calories of beef jerky, or approximately one 1/4 ounce stick. The difference is dramatic.

How many more people could be fed if less of us ate meat? "According to a report from the Feinstein World Hunger Program at Brown University, if the world's food supply were distributed equally among all people so that every one received the United Nations-recommended intake of 2,350 calories per day, primarily from grains, there would be enough food for 6 billion people. But if 10% of the calories came from animal sources, as in the average South American diet, only 4 billion people could be sustained. And if 30% of the calories were from animal sources, only 2.5 billion people could be fed." (Global Tomorrow Coalition, 1990)

"Of the 145 million tons of grain and soy fed to our beef cattle, poultry, and hogs in 1979, only 21 million tons were returned to us in meat, poultry, and eggs. The rest, about 124 million tons of grain and soybeans, became inaccessible to human consumption...To put this enormous quantity in some perspective, consider that 120 million tons is worth over $20 billion. If cooked, it is the equivalent of 1 cup of grain for every single human being on earth every day for a year." —Francis Moore Lappé

The following statistics are from *67 Ways to Save the Animals* by Anna Sequoia and are drawn from *Diet for a New America* by John Robbins and *Animal Factories* by Jim Mason and Peter Singer:
— 85% of the 4 million acres of topsoil lost in the United States each year is directly related to the raising of livestock.
— More than half the water consumed in the United States each year is used in factory (animal) farming.
— 260 million acres of oxygen-producing trees have been cut down to create cropland to produce a meat-centered diet.
— Production of a single pound of meat requires 2,500 gallons of water. A pound of wheat can be produced with just 25 gallons.
— 95% of the oats grown in this country are eaten by livestock. 80% of the corn grown here is eaten by livestock. 90% of its value as protein is wasted by cycling grain through livestock.
— Factory farm animals produce 250,000 pounds of excrement each sec-

ond. Much of that winds up, untreated, in our streams and lakes—and in our groundwater.

— The tropical rainforests of Central and South America, home to half of all the living species on earth, are being decimated to produce hamburger meat for fast-food restaurants. This loss of rainforest is responsible for most of the 1,000 species extinction each year.

FOLLOW-UP, MAIN ACTIVITY: Remind the group that these numbers refer to **average** caloric intake. The poorest 20% receives far less than the average. "Each year an estimated 40-60 million people die from hunger and hunger-related disease." (Global Tomorrow Coalition, 1990)

Background: Global Food Issues
—from Ed Passerini's *The Curve of the Future.* Used with permission

How did we get to this strange time and place? How did we get to a world of five billion people, many of whom go to bed hungry each night?

About 10,000 years ago, humankind began its present drive to increase population by changing its eating habits. About 10,000 years ago, the hunter-gatherers discovered how to plant seeds and harvest plants. Primarily, we learned how to cultivate three species of grasses—rice, wheat, and corn—and these three grains continue to this day to feed most of humankind. "All flesh is grass." Around the same time, we learned to herd nine main species of animals, all of them birds or mammals. These nine—cattle,

John Heine

sheep, goats, water buffalo, pigs, chicken, turkey, geese, and ducks—continue to provide us with most of our animal protein...

Humankind is different from wild animals. Wild animals usually eat only 2 or 3% of their potential food supply before their population comes under control. Wild mammals have built-in mechanisms that cause them to limit their population size after they have eaten only a small portion of their food supply—all the mammals except us—**we** are no longer wild...Human beings eat right up to the edge of the food supply and then try to supply more food rather than to curb population. We are covering the Earth with our farms. We eat more than all the wild mammals combined. And many people are hungry because we eat right up to and beyond our limits. What are those limits? The easy answer is that we could feed as many as **8 billion** people today if we really put a lot of effort into it. Many of them wouldn't be very well fed, and the stress on the world's soil would be terrifying, but we could probably do it for a short time...

Although we **might** be able to feed up to 8 billion people **today**, we may **not** be able to sustain as many as **4 billion** in the future because of eroded soil, etc. The reason is that it takes about 2 1/2 acres per person to supply a minimally adequate diet. About **one** acre per person will feed perhaps half of the population decently, while the other half suffers. But at most, 7.8 billion acres of land on this planet can be farmed. We already farm about 4.5 billion acres and recent studies say that it is unlikely that we will be able to bring into production a total of more than 6 or 7 billion acres. And this acreage is already eroding at an alarming rate...

The arable land available to **agriculture** continues to decrease. This is because industries and cities compete for that land as population grows, and also because of physical reasons such as erosion, salting, chronic drought, etc.

The best land is **already** being farmed, and even this best land requires fertilizer and irrigation to get the high yields we expect. The land that we open up in the next 20 years with genetically improved grains will require a much higher investment of fertilizers and energy. This new land is typically low in humus content, tilth, and crumb structure; it will be difficult to plow and difficult to keep from eroding. Even the excellent soils of the United States are eroding rapidly. The average acre of Iowa corn land loses over 9 tons of topsoil each year. Eventually, it will all flow to the sea if something is not done...

There are temporary expedients that can marginally reduce the hunger of the poorest—we can distribute land and food better, stop eating grain-fed cattle, and stop feeding so much to pets (In 1988, there were 107 million pet dogs and cats in the United States)—they eat more than our children eat. But the ultimate problem is the conflict between human food needs and poor land.

Americans often claim that "if the people of India would just **eat** their cows rather than worship them, everything would be fine." However, the people of India have tabooed the killing of cows for significant reasons: cows give milk, reproduce themselves, provide their own fuel by eating high-cellulose grasses that human beings can't eat, pull plows, drop fertilizer, and are even brought into the house on cold nights! (A cow is the equivalent of a 1000-watt heater.) Killing a cow is like killing the goose that lays golden eggs!

A more interesting proposal is the Indian suggestion that Americans do away with many of their 107 million cats and dogs, which contribute **nothing** to food or agriculture and yet consume vast quantities of fairly high-quality food. (In 1980 the U.S. cat food market was three times the size of the babyfood market.)...Certainly, no one would urge you to go blow Ol' Shep's brains out, but once Ol' Shep has naturally passed on, you might consider **not** replacing him. Pets are nice companions, but we **can** live without them...The problem is that we have not just a **human** population explosion, but an explosion of people **and** their dependents (cows, cats, dogs, rats, etc.). Before long, we must begin to stem the population growth of all of them.

> The causal chain of the deterioration [of the environment] is easily followed to its source. Too many cars, too many factories, too much detergent, too much pesticide, multiplying contrails, inadequate sewage treatment plants, too little water, too much carbon dioxide — all can be traced easily to too many people.
> —Paul R. Ehrlich

The Numbers Game

Time Required	20 minutes
Group Size	10 or more
Materials	Yarn or cord, dried beans, whistle
Location	Spacious
Indoor Use	Yes
Intended Result	Fuller comprehension of the population issue

SUMMARY: Students play a game with beans to illustrate the effects of population on resources.

PREPARATION: Review the background material at the end of the activity and decide how much of it is appropriate to share with your group.

PROCEDURE: Make a large circle on the ground with the yarn or cord. Scatter half a bag of beans inside the circle. Several students move into the circle—they represent the population of the planet before 1850. The remaining students stand outside the circle. At a signal (whistle), the students pick up a bean (or a specified number of beans) and either put it in their pockets or return it to a central location. These are resources that have been used and are no longer available.

Increase the population. Put half of the remaining beans in the circle to represent the discovery and increased exploitation of additional resources. The increased population not only needs more beans, they use more beans per capita, so increase the number they have to pick up.

Put everyone in the circle and put in the remaining beans. Point out that all major resources are now either used or discovered and no more resources can be added. Again, have the students pick up beans at the signal. When someone can't reach her quota of beans in any round, she must leave the circle. Let the numbers reduce until two, one, or even no one is left in the circle.

NOTES: If too many beans are in the circle, increase the number that each student must pick up during each round. No hoarding allowed.

VARIATIONS:
1. Begin in the 20th century and let everyone join the circle from the start.
2. Make the circle very large. Let roughly 1/3 of the students represent the industrialized world. They can move around freely and must collect four beans at the signal. The 2/3 representing the non-industrialized world

only pick up one bean at the signal (rather than four), but they must sit and pick up only beans that they can reach without leaving their position. [The activity and variations were adapted from "A Teacher's Guide to Environmental Education," published by The Alabama Environmental Council. Used with permission.]

Background: Population
—from Edward Passerini's *The Curve of the Future*. Used with permission.

During most of the time people have lived on Earth, there have been very few of us—and we've led a pretty precarious existence. But we slowly learned how to control our food supply, and the human population began to grow and—ever so slowly—the rate of growth began to speed up. Now, suddenly, we find ourselves with an exploding population.

Less than 150 years ago—in 1850—we didn't even have one billion people on Earth. But 80 years later—by 1930—we had TWO billion! In those 80 years we added as many people to the living world population as we had added in the hundreds of thousands of years before 1850.

Between 1930 and 1960 we added another billion people—it took only **30 years** for the third billion. Between 1960 and 1975, only **15** years, we produced a fourth. If you have, say, only a few million people, it takes a long time to breed a billion more. But if you already have five billion, it doesn't take long to breed another billion. How long? About twelve years. And the next billion? Hard to say. How many more people can the Earth take? What can we do? What should we do?...

Although no one knows exactly what the eventual population of the Earth will be, we can make some pretty good guesses. Biologists Paul Ehrlich and Jacques-Yves Cousteau now estimate that we can't sustain more than 2 billion people once our "fossil" resources run out. A sustainable organic agriculture based on renewable water (i.e., rainwater, after our fossil, underground water supplies are exhausted) will support between one billion and two billion people.

But if we all want more than just food, we will need renewable timberland for furniture, **even if we make all our houses out of inert** (i.e., nonliving) **materials** such as rock or brick or rammed earth or adobe. And if we want many consumer goods—even long-lasting consumer goods—the population will have to be quite low. For example, for a world population to have as much aluminum to use as the 200 million people in the U.S. have, the world population could be only about 1/2 billion. The figure for steel is about 0.7 billion. If we consume at the more moderate levels of the Europeans, the figure rises by perhaps 80%. Perhaps, to be safe, we should figure on about 2 billion people as a **maximum**. One billion would be safer...

Psychologist John Calhoun built a large bin (9 feet in diameter) and provided it with a continuous supply of food, water, and nesting materials. He also built in 260 cozy little "dens." He then put four pairs of mice inside and waited to see what would happen. The mice multiplied normally and happily up to about 150 mice. But as the numbers increased up toward about 600, a few odd behavior patterns began to creep in. By the time this little "mouse planet" had reached 600, the **maximum population growth rate** was reached, but the population continued to expand until it reached a horrendous 2,200, and then the behavior of the mice can only be described as insane. Unprovoked violence, extreme passivity, cannibalism, and aberrant sexual and territorial behavior became common. The death rates were very high, and the mice simply lost their ability to cope with their environment. The population began to plummet. Calhoun stopped the experiment at the point where none of the females could produce babies any longer — the population of the "mouse planet" was headed toward extinction.

We should be careful about drawing too many conclusions from Calhoun's work, but a number of scientists (including Calhoun) are worried. Calhoun believes that many of the signs of aberrant behaviors which showed up in the mice are now showing up in humans. He matched the curve of population growth for the "mouse-planet" to the curve for humans on the Earth and concluded that if the Earth reaches a population of about **9 billion people**, we will have crossed a kind of threshold from which there is no return...Most scientists scoff at such a "pessimistic" scenario, but the parallels between the "mouse planet" and our own are unsettling. And since it is now clear that a growing population is against our best interests and that a reduction of population promotes a higher quality of life, we should begin to get (and keep) our birth rate down much lower than it is now. Most current projections show that the Earth's population could reach 10 billion in the next century. Herman Kahn says 15 billion...By contrast, Lester Brown and the low-side U.N. projections say that we could, if we act fast, peak at 8 billion or below.

It is worth noting that the mouse population in Calhoun's tank never did get up to the **maximum physical carrying capacity** of the tank. Calhoun believes that the mice became mentally incapable of coping with the changes they made in their environment. Extending the results of his experiment to the human population of the Earth, Calhoun believes that anything over 9 billion would be disaster, that anything between 8 and 9 billion would result in a world in which people have lost much of their will to live, and much of the human creative spirit. He feels that if the human peak occurs at about 6 billion, that we can recover easily.

What's The Connection?

Time Required	15 minutes or longer
Group Size	Any
Materials	None
Location	Anywhere
Indoor Use	Yes
Intended Result	Awareness of connections between daily life and the rest of the world

SUMMARY: The group explores the connections between their own lives and the resources, people, agriculture, and industry of the world.

PREPARATION: Understand some of these connections yourself. Read the background information at the end of the activity.

PROCEDURE: Ask a student to point out an article of clothing; then let the crew or class brainstorm to figure out how it came from the earth. For example, a shirt might be named. The first response might be tracing the cotton in the shirt to the plant which grew in the earth. You ask, "But what about the button?" and allow more complex connections through petroleum and plant and/or animal life to emerge. Then what about the dye, and the wrapping the shirt came in, and the pins or tape that held it together? And what pathways did all these materials travel to come together to be present in this place? Whose labor went into it? What machinery was used, and where did the components of the machines come from? Where will the shirt go when the wearer is finished with it? (In most cities fiber can be recycled by Goodwill Industries or a similar organization.)

Remind the group how the processes involved in the production of the shirt and other items all connect eventually to the earth.

BACKGROUND: In "Journey of the Blouse," John Cavanagh of the Institute for Policy Studies explores some of the pathways that might contribute to the making of a 35% cotton/65% polyester blouse. The cotton was grown on an El Salvador plantation, where the workers are not protected

There's part of every living person that is three and a half billion years old.
— David Brower

against pesticide sprayings and where they are paid around $2 per day. The cotton is then shipped by Cargill through the Panama Canal to a port in South Carolina and sold to Burlington. Burlington loads the cotton into trucks and transports it to a South Carolina spinning mill.

Meanwhile, oil for the polyester is pumped in Venezuela. Workers there have little safety protection and make around $6 per day. Venezuela sells the oil to Exxon, which takes it to Trinidad and Tobago for refining. The refined oil is loaded onto another ship and travels to New Jersey. Trucks carry it to DuPont, where the oil is converted into filament.

The filament goes to Burlington, North Carolina, and the cotton comes from South Carolina to the same textile plant. The two products are combined and woven on power looms into rolls of fabric. Sears buys the cloth and ships it to Haiti, where it is transported to small sweatshops. Women there work long days for $3 a day. Even discussing the prospect of forming a union means dismissal.

The finished blouses come to New York, are sealed in plastic and sent all over the United States.

A copy of the full article can be obtained from the Institute for Policy Studies, 1601 Connecticut Ave. NW, Washington, D.C. 20009. The musical group, Sweet Honey in the Rock used the article to write their song "Are My Hands Clean?"

Going Further: Students can research where items which they commonly wear or use are manufactured. Where appropriate, they can write letters either commending or questioning the manufacturing process.

When it came time to buy new running shoes, writer Sallie Tisdale began calling shoe companies to see which were still using Asian labor to make their shoes. The answer: all of them. The problem: most shoe makers in Southeast Asia are teenagers; fifteen to sixteen hour days can earn less than $1.80 per day. Two companies, Nike and Reebok, make almost all of their shoes in Southeast Asia. Best on the list was New Balance, which makes 70% of its shoes in the United States, with shoe makers earning $10 to $12 per hour plus benefits. Tisdale went with the New Balance and found that the shoes were "comfortable in several different ways."

(Sallie Tisdale's article first appeared
in *The New Republic*.)

Not In My Backyard

Time Required	20-30 minutes
Group Size	8-15
Materials	Clean used paper
Location	Any
Indoor Use	Yes
Intended Result	Increased awareness of garbage problems and recycling as a solution

SUMMARY: Not in My Backyard is a game whereby students work to avoid having garbage dumped on them.

PREPARATION: Take 50 sheets of used paper, preferably used on one side. Write on each sheet of paper.

On 20 sheets of paper write: Paper—40%
On 9 sheets of paper write: Yard Waste—18%
On 4 sheets of paper write: Food Waste—8%
On 4 sheets of paper write: Plastic—8%
On 4 sheets of paper write: Glass—8%
On 5 sheets of paper write: Metals—10%
On 4 sheets of paper write: Other—8%

Crumple them up separately so that the words you've written don't show.

PROCEDURE: Each person represents a community in the same area of the state. All of the communities generate garbage and need to bury it somewhere. But where?

The communities are adjacent to one another. Surrounding them is an area of 4 major plots of cropland, 2 parks, 3 areas of forest land, 1 dairy farm.

The people sit in a circle and the instructor hands a piece of trash to every third person. The group begins to sing (to the tune of "London Bridge is Falling Down"), "Don't put your trash in my backyard, my backyard, my backyard, Don't put your trash in my backyard, My backyard is full." Or they might be more comfortable chanting, "Not in my backyard, Hey, Not in my backyard, Hey." At a signal, the singing or chanting stops, and the people holding the trash place it in front of them. Three new pieces are handed in and the song begins again. This continues until 1 community (person) has 2 pieces of trash.

Now this community must find a place to bury the trash and must build a landfill from one of the available parks, farms, or forests. The landfill can hold six loads of trash (with two pieces per load). When it's full and another community fills up, a new landfill has to be found. But at this point tell the students that there is no more land to spare, they've got to find a better way.

Take all of the trash and divide it as equally as possible among the students. Have them open the paper to find out what kind of trash they have. Ask them if what they have can be recycled. Every sheet of paper represents 2% of the waste stream and gives the total percentage of the waste stream for that particular item. Everything except Other can theoretically be recycled or composted. What problems have to be overcome in order for more recycling to occur?

To have what we want is riches, but to be able to do without is power.

—George MacDonald

Life on this earth is not about consuming as much as we can afford, but about some very simple things, which can be expressed in very simple words like:

Do for others what you want others to do for you;
Love your neighbor as you love yourself;
Prove all things; hold fast that which is good.

Why beat about the bush? This is what life is about.

—E.F. Schumacher

Private Landfill

Time Required	Part of a three day outing
Group Size	Any
Materials	Garbage sacks
Location	Outdoors
Indoor Use	Yes (variations)
Intended Result	First-hand appreciation of garbage problems

DESCRIPTION: Each person carries her own garbage for 3 days.

Everywhere the crew members go (to the bathroom, to bed, etc.) they carry the garbage with them in a bag. They must also decide what to do with group-generated garbage.
    As a variation, each person can carry someone else's trash.

OPTION: If the outing is 9 days, trash can be measured 3 days before, during, and three days after the activity. Is there a difference?

FOLLOW-UP:
1. The group can go through the garbage and discuss potential recyclables.
2. The group should discuss how they feel about having the garbage so close all of the time. Did anyone like having garbage next to them? Would anyone like living next to a landfill? Did anyone's bag leak? What happens when a landfill leaks?
3. How did the group deal with group trash? Who got it and why?
4. Did this activity make a difference to anyone?
5. Did anyone come up with solutions that would reduce the amount of trash generated? Source reduction is an increasingly compelling alternative to landfilling, incinerating, and recycling.

DISCUSSION:
1. How much garbage does each of us produce? How much less could we produce? How do individual students cope with garbage in their own homes?
2. How do landfills work? Incinerators? Recycling centers? What problems do each have?
3. What is Household Hazardous Waste, and what can we do about it?

VARIATION (Indoors):
Each Student can carry her non-food trash with her everywhere she goes at school. This can go on for one day, several days, or even several weeks.

Students get an idea of what they generate. Group trash might include what's generated by the school's office. At the end of the period, materials can be sorted into recyclables and non-recyclables.

Background: Garbage.

Garbage is a complicated issue. Most Americans know that we produce around 4 pounds of garbage per person per day without realizing that refers only to "municipal solid waste," defined as household and commercial trash only. We produce an equivalent amount of construction and demolition debris, about 4 pounds per person per day. Industry produces about 8 pounds per person per day of hazardous waste. But industry also produces around 12 pounds per person per day of industrial garbage that is non-hazardous.

Then there is wastewater (what we flush, what industry flushes), waste that is released into the air (more than 2.5 pounds per person per day, not counting the more than 40 pounds per person per day of carbon dioxide), medical waste, radioactive waste, military waste, mining and milling waste, agricultural waste (including animal carcasses, pesticide runoff, herbicide and fertilizer runoff, and even topsoil).

Household garbage makes up around 1% of the waste our society produces. And what is waste? In the natural world, waste is a resource for another lifeform. But in the quantities, types, and concentrations people

John Heine

produce it, waste can be a poison; waste can be something that could have been reused but wasn't; waste can be a residue of the process of "wasting" (in the sense of "laying waste to") the natural world.

Waste is a pervasive environmental problem not only because it poisons the environment directly, but also because it wastes resources. As we throw away resources with one hand, we reach out to the natural world with the other and continue to grab, use, and abuse the resources that remain. We continue to deprive other creatures of habitat, cut old growth forest, and stripmine land in large part because of the ways we handle our garbage and other wastes.

Because the problem of waste is so large and so pervasive, there is no solution that doesn't create problems of its own. Landfilling, incineration, and recycling are all extremely expensive; all are potential polluters; all use a lot of transportation energy. The problem with landfilling is not that we're running out of land—we have plenty of land (though we might decide that there are better uses for it). The problems with landfilling are: it wastes resources by burying them; it produces methane gas which pollutes the air and helps render the land unsuitable for any other use; and it mixes small amounts of toxic material with large amounts of untoxic material to make a toxic soup that will have to be dealt with by future generations.

Even though incinerators produce energy, they do not begin to capture the energy that went into making the products they consume, energy that can only be redeemed by reusing or recycling. Incinerators pollute the air and produce toxic ash unless the garbage is carefully separated, which increases the expense. Once built, incinerators must be fed, taking away opportunities for innovative reuse and recycling technologies.

Recycling also has plenty of problems, including recycling industries that pollute, market gluts, lack of interest, lack of participation, and expense. But if done right, recycling is environmentally sound, produces relatively little waste, and saves significantly more resources than the other two options. Recycling technology continues to improve and expand. Curbside recycling is an inefficient use of garbage dollars, which could be better used to recycle industrial and commercial waste and compost the 25% of garbage that is yard and food wastes. But curbside recycling remains an important education and outreach tool that empowers people by giving them the opportunity to save resources.

Source reduction remains the untapped opportunity for dealing with garbage. "Waste that isn't generated in the first place doesn't have to be burned, buried, or dumped at sea. Waste that isn't generated in the first place doesn't squander natural resources." (Quote from INFORM's 1993 Annual Report). (Other information from The Alabama Environmental Council. Used with permission.)

World View Drawings

Time Required	2 hours
Group Size	Any
Materials	Paper and drawing materials (see below)
Location	Any
Indoor Use	Yes
Intended Result	Increased awareness, through self-expression and communication, of our place in the world

SUMMARY: Students use drawing to represent, illustrate, express their place in the world.

PREPARATION: Before quiet time, ask participants to think about their place in the world. How do they fit in? What guides their choices in life? What's important?

PROCEDURE: If Possible, give each student the opportunity to spend time alone. Time on a "solo" in the outdoors, out of sight of other people, might last anywhere from fifteen minutes to several hours (on Outward Bound courses a solo may last as long as three days.) If circumstance doen't allow students to be alone, have them spend 30 minutes of quiet time together.

After students have had time to think, bring them together and talk briefly about symbols. Letters, figures, colors can represent something else. Ask students to draw their place in the world using symbols. This should be done silently, each person working on her own. If they want to use words, invite them to put the words on the opposite side of the page.

Ask each person to talk about her world. She may use her picture if she wants to. The important thing is to talk about her world and her place in the world.

The Shrinking Outdoors

Time Required	15 minutes
Group Size	Any
Materials	Drawing materials, natural if possible
Location	Outdoors, near the end of a course or outdoor immersion
Indoor Use	Yes
Intended Result	Commitment to spend more time in natural settings

SUMMARY: Students calculate where they usually spend their time, outdoors versus indoors.

PROCEDURE: At the end of an extended period in the out-of-doors, many students will have connected with the beauty and wonder of the outdoors on a new level. It is a good time for them to consider, perhaps using a stick to calculate in bare earth, or using charred wood for chalk and sections of bark for tablet, how much time they usually spend outdoors. Explain to students that they will make their estimates based on a typical week at home. (This activity can also be adapted for indoors.)

Ask students to draw a large circle.

Ask them to calculate what percentage of their time they spend inside buildings. This includes working, sleeping, and indoor eating and recreation. Have them mark that percentage on their circle. The remaining segment will almost certainly be less than half of the circle.

Of the remaining time, how much is spent in automobiles? Have students mark that off.

Of the remaining segment, how much of the time outdoors is spent on pavement or other artificial surfaces. Mark that off. Of the time remaining, how much is spent in a domesticated environment. For most students the entire circle will be filled by now.

Compare that circle with one for the course or intensive time outdoors. Compare it with the way people spent their time 10,000 years ago, 1,000 years ago, 100 years ago. People were designed to spend time outdoors.

Ask students to think of advantages of spending time outdoors. Emphasize the rewards. Invite students to join you in making a conscious commitment to spend more time outdoors, whether it be on porches, in yards or parks, or in the wild. Invite them to make a commitment to stretch their horizons by spending more time in wild areas.

The Human Circle

Time Required	60 minutes or longer
Group Size	8 to 15
Materials	4 natural objects for directions, compass
Location	Outdoors
Indoor Use	Yes
Intended Result	Greater respect for nature, greater respect for Native Americans, clearer understanding of having a place in the human circle

SUMMARY: Using a Medicine Wheel, participants are given the opportunity to find their own place in the human circle.

PREPARATION: Have four stones or other natural objects to place at the four major points of the compass. Their colors will be yellow (East), green (South), brown (West), and white (North).

Familiarize yourself with the descriptions of the four directions (below) and with any other information you have on the Medicine Wheel. The less you work from notes on this activity, the better your presentation will be.

PROCEDURE: Students should know that what they are doing is a variation on a Native American Medicine Wheel. Native Americans have expressed concern that their spiritual beliefs and practices are being distorted and usurped by Americans of European descent and others.

Communicate to your students that Native American spirituality inspired the activity. Because the activity reflects another set of cultural beliefs and values, it must be approached with respect. At the same time, however, it is not a Native American ceremony and does not pretend to be.

Mark off an area of a circle about two yards in diameter. First, place the yellow object at the easternmost point of the circle and describe the qualities of this direction. Proceed clockwise, placing the green object in the south, brown in the west, and white in the north. Describe the qualities of each direction as the object is placed:

EAST—the place where things begin; sunrise, springtime, spirituality, illumination, seeing the big picture, inspiration, creativity. The eagle lives here seeing small things from far away.

SOUTH—innocence; summertime; feelings and emotions honored; human relations are nurtured; process is highly valued. The mouse lives in the south and cares for her family.

WEST—introspective, rational, analytical, thinks critically and linearly; autumn. The bear lives here, hibernating and thinking.

NORTH—assertive, active, physical, wise, likes challenges, endures hardship, courageous; high level of task orientation. The buffalo lives in the arduous north plodding on through thick and thin.

Relate that all parts of the circle are important and necessary to make the whole. The directions are different yet of equal value. The directions balance one another.

Ask students to spend a few minutes thinking about where they have been in the circle. Then ask them to move to their direction in the circle. They can stand behind a cardinal direction or anywhere on the continuum between two directions. Ask students to describe how they see themselves in that place. To celebrate the person, everyone verbally affirms each one who finds his or her place in the circle. The Lakota Sioux affirmation is warm, heartfelt, "Ho!"

VARIATIONS:
1. Ask students to identify world figures with the characteristics of each direction or to identify where on the wheel they think specific world figures should go.
2. As a feedback exercise, have students place each other in the circle.
3. Begin by asking students to go to that place on the circle which represents where they see themselves in their lives (as opposed to where they want to be). Then ask them to move to that place on the circle which represents where they would like to be.

NATIVE AMERICANS SPEAK:
Black Elk, 1932: You have noticed that everything an Indian does is in a circle, and that is because the Power of the World always works in circles, and everything tries to be round. In the old days when we were a strong and happy people, all our power came to us from the sacred hoop of the nation, and so long as the hoop was unbroken, the people flourished. The flowering tree was the living center of the hoop, and the circle of the four quarters nourished it. The east gave peace and light, the south gave warmth, the west gave rain, and the north with its cold and mighty wind gave strength and endurance. This knowledge came to us from the outer world with our religion. Everything the Power of the World does is done in a circle. The sky is round, and I have heard that the earth is round like a ball, and so are all the stars. The wind, in its greatest power, whirls. Birds make their nests in circles, for theirs is the same religion as ours. The sun comes forth and goes down again in a circle. The moon does the same, and

both are round. Even the seasons form a great circle in their changing, and always come back again to where they were.

Luther Standing Bear, 1933: The old people came literally to love the soil and they sat or reclined on the ground with a feeling of being close to a mothering power. It was good for the skin to touch the earth and the old people liked to remove their moccasins and walk with bare feet on the sacred earth.

Luther Standing Bear: Knowledge was inherent in all things. The world was a library and its books were the stones, leaves, grass, brooks, and the birds and animals that shared, alike with us, the storms and blessings of earth.

Luther Standing Bear: Indian boys, who are naturally reared, are alert to their surroundings; their senses are not narrowed to observing only one another, and they cannot spend hours seeing nothing, hearing nothing, and thinking nothing in particular. Observation was certain in its rewards; interest, wonder, admiration grew, and the fact was appreciated that life was more than mere human manifestation; that it was expressed in a multitude of forms. This appreciation enriched Lakota existence. Life was vivid and pulsing; nothing was casual and commonplace. The Indian lived—lived in every sense of the word—from his first to his last breath.

Sitting Bull, 1868: I wish all to know that I do not propose to sell any part of my country, nor will I have the whites cutting our timber along the rivers, more especially the oak. I am particularly fond of the little groves of oak trees. I love to look at them, and feel a reverence for them, because they endure the wintry storm and summer's heat, and not like ourselves, seem to thrive and flourish in them.

Tecumseh, Shawnee chief, in 1810, protesting the partition of land: No tribe has the right to sell, even to each other, much less to strangers...Sell a country! Why not sell the air, the great sea, as well as the earth? Did not the Great Spirit make them all for the use of his children.

Terra Manasco, Anglo Southerner and Chickamauga Cherokee, writing in *The Bankhead Monitor*, 1993:
    Can you feel the close-in creeping of the green around you, the air heavy with water and spirits, the canyons deep and winding, the voices of my ancestors chanting as they walked the Rainbow, the roar of the waterfalls that carry the voice of Thunder?
    Can you pool now like plasma in the secret sinuses of the Southern Heart? Will you dance with me in the fairy ring deep in the forest while the

old ones watch? Can you mimic the cry of the falcon that breaks free of its cage? There, just beneath the sound of your own breath, can you hear the song of the little mysteries? Can you see the tiny geometries take shape in the grit of the canyon floor as the wind spins in four directions? If you walked here with me, would you know that you walk in a forest where even the plants are warriors? And in this heart, can you hear your own blood singing? And if you walked across this land, would you cry for the Turtle from the depths of your heart?

I think that you would feel all of these things...Are we not, after all, one spirit, in a world without boundaries? Are we not, after all—you, I and all creatures—the genetic prayers of the Great Mystery? Yes? Then the time has come for all of us to make New Medicine, to create new stories faster than the Destroyers can end them, to protect the sacred for Those Who Come and to cherish all things which must be kept. I have spoken. <u>Ah ho</u>, it is so.

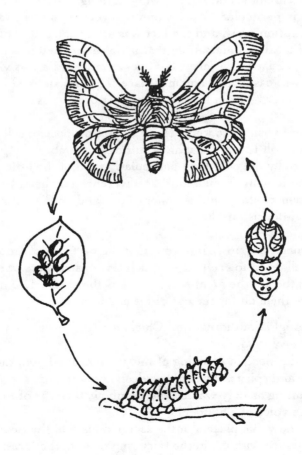

Going Further: Global & Local

1. **Write your elected officials**...Express your concerns about environmental issues as individuals or as a class or group. If possible, write about specific legislation, identifying the name and number of the bill. Be brief and courteous. Write elected officials to ask if they have joined **GLOBE (Global Legislators Organization for a Balanced Environment)**. GLOBE encourages communication on environmental issues among governments around the world. It focuses on issues of climate change, biodiversity, forests, international institutions, trade, and the environment. If your officials have not joined, encourage them to. GLOBE International, Director: Lena Lindahl; Ginza Form 21 Bldg. 7th Floor; Ginza 8-18-4; Chuo-ku, Tokyo 104 Japan. GLOBE USA, Director: Patrick Ramage; 4409 3rd Street SW, Suite 204; Washington DC 20024.

In the United States write the president at The White House, 1600 Pennsylvania Avenue NW, Washington, DC 20500. Write "Dear Mr. President..."

Write your Senator at U.S. Senate, Washington, DC 20515

Write your Representative at U.S. House of Representatives, same address. Your heading should be addressed to The Honorable _____, your salutation should read Dear Senator _____ or Dear Representative _____.

2. **Take a look at your institution's food**...EarthSave is publishing a *Healthy People Healthy Planet Action Guide* for people who want to work with schools for food-related education and more environmentally sound food service choices—HPHP, c/o EarthSave, 706 Frederick Street, Santa Cruz, CA 95062.

3. **Grade your the environmental performance of your school, workplace, church**...The Environmental Report Card which follows is a starting point for greater environmental awareness. Participants can think of more areas to assess, more things to monitor, and further creative ways to communicate an environmental perspective to other students, employees and staff.

An Environmental Report Card

You can get started working with your fellow students, teachers, and school staff to improve your school's environment. Your first step, using this Environmental Report Card, is to evaluate your school's present performance.

Every school is a small community of its own. Schools create and dispose of garbage, contain potentially toxic materials, and use energy. This report card allows you to identify whether your school employs...environmentally sound practices.

There are many opportunities for environmental action throughout your school: in classrooms, the cafeteria, the kitchen, and other areas. In each area, the kinds of good environmental steps that can be taken correspond to a "yes" answer to the questions below. Your goal is to see how many of these steps your school has taken and to identify the ones it has not yet taken—but could consider.

Answer yes or no for each question. If you don't understand why one of the steps listed is a good one to take, discuss it with other students or your teacher and find out why before you mark this sheet.

Then you can add up your school's total grade. After you have filled in each blank, give your school three points for each "yes" (99 is the highest possible score). You'll have a clearer picture of how well your school is doing and ways to make it more environmentally committed.

Classrooms   **Yes or No**

Are both sides of paper used for classwork?   _____

Are scraps used for notepaper?   _____

Are there separate containers for paper recycling?   _____

Are disposable items, such as pens and markers,
   discouraged?   _____

Is energy-efficient fluorescent lighting used?   _____

Are lights turned off when not in use?   _____

Are there plants to improve indoor air quality?   _____

Cafeteria   **Yes or No**

Are there designated recycling bins for aluminum,
   paper waste, and food waste?   _____

Cafeteria (continued)   **Yes or No**

Are beverage dispensers provided instead of individual
   cartons?   _____

Are there washable, reusable trays, plates, bowls,
   glasses, and utensils?   _____

Kitchen

Yes or No

Are cans, bottles, and plastics from food preparation
    recycled? _____

Are food scraps emptied into a school compost pile? _____

Are nontoxic dishwashing and cleaning products used? _____

Are either cloth or 100% recycled paper towels used? _____

Bathrooms

Yes or No

Are there water-conserving tanks in the toilets? _____

Are there cloth rolls, air dryers, or 100% recycled paper
    towels? _____

Custodial Services

Yes or No

Are hazardous wastes (oil, paint, cleaners) disposed of
    properly? _____

Are yard materials composted? _____

Are used cardboard boxes recycled? _____

Are the least toxic pest control methods used? _____

Are nontoxic cleaners used? _____

Is energy conserved by turning off lights, air conditioners,
    and radiators when not in use? _____

Teachers' Lounge

Yes or No

Are coffee grounds collected for composting? _____

Are there recycling bins? _____

Are there mugs for each teacher instead of disposables
    and sugar bowls rather than individual packets? _____

Office/Administration

Yes or No

Is recycled paper used for all printing and correspondence? _____

Are announcements posted rather than duplicated for staff? _____

Are letters and class materials copied on both sides? _____

Are the backs of telephone message slips reused for notes? _____

Is everyone encouraged to use paper recycling bins? _____

Student Activities

Yes or No

Is group transportation provided to conserve energy? _____

Are school publications printed on recycled paper? _____

Is the student government active in promoting recycling
    and other environmental projects? _____

Each "yes" is worth three points. Add up the score to find out your school's environmental grade and what you can do next.

87-99 Your school is off to a good start in cleaning up its own act. Look for new areas to make an impact.

72-84 Your school has room to improve. Investigate the areas marked "no" to find positive steps your school could take.

Below 72 Your school needs a remedial course in environmental awareness. A good place to start is waste reduction and recycling, but any of the areas with "no" marks will do.

Good Luck!

EarthNotes: Global and Local

"Poverty, malnutrition, and health ailments currently afflict more than 1 billion people worldwide. Every day, over 800 million people go hungry, many of them children. Some 1.5 billion people do not have access to basic health care and are threatened by a host of diseases, many of them easily avoidable." (Sitarz, 1993)

"The world's population reached 5.5 billion in mid-1992. Of these 77% lived in developing countries and 23% in industrialized countries...It is projected that the world population will reach some 6.3 billion people in the year 2000 and 8.5 billion in the year 2025." (Sitarz, 1993)

"Approximately 1/3 of the world's population are children under 15 years old. At least 15 million of these children die each year from preventable diseases." (Sitarz, 1993)

"Compared to the rest of the world, the developed nations consume 12 times more energy, 10 times more steel, and 15 times more paper." (Stead & Stead, 1992)

"About four of every five miles traveled by Americans is by car." (Makower, 1992)

"Americans send enough aluminum to landfills every three months to rebuild the U.S. commercial air fleet." (Stead & Stead, 1992)

"By increasing gas mileage to 45 miles per gallon in cars and 35 miles per gallon in small trucks... 2.8 million barrels of oil a day could be saved. This is more than the United States currently acquires from the Middle East and the Alaskan pipeline combined." (Stead & Stead, 1992)

Garbage per capita per year in kilograms:		
	United States	864
	Switzerland	424
	Japan	394
	United Kingdom	357
	Sweden	317

(Source: World Resources Institute)

Readings: Global and Local

We stand now where two roads diverge. But unlike the roads in Robert Frost's familiar poem, they are not equally fair. The road we have long been traveling is deceptively easy, a smooth superhighway on which we progress with great speed, but at its end lies disaster. The other fork of the road—the one "less traveled by"—offers our last, our only chance to reach a destination that assures the preservation of our earth.
—Rachel Carson

If anything's easy, it's not likely to be worthwhile.
—Hubert Humphrey

For the first time in history, humanity must face the risk of unintentionally destroying the foundations of life on Earth. The global scientific consensus is that if the current levels of environmental deterioration continue, the delicate life-sustaining qualities of this planet will collapse.
—Daniel Sitarz

I am convinced that once we pass beyond the mere awareness of impending disaster and begin to understand why we have come to the present predicament, and where the alternative paths ahead can lead, there is reason to find in the very depths of the environmental crisis itself a source of optimism.
—Barry Commoner

"I am protecting the rainforest" develops to "I am part of the rainforest protecting myself. I am that part of the rainforest recently emerged into thinking." What a relief then! The thousands of years of imagined separation are over and we being to recall our true nature. That is, the change is a spiritual one, thinking like a mountain, sometimes referred to as "deep ecology."
—John Seed

We homo sapiens are recent arrivals on this planet, and we should have just a little bit of humility.
—David Brower

You can't run a throwaway society on a finite planet.
—Paul Connett

We have tamed the wilderness only to discover we have made it less habitable and less beautiful in the process.
—Dan Meyer

I would like to go back to the time of Moses and say, "Go back up and bring back down the other tablet!" The Ten Commandments just talk about how we're supposed to treat each other. There's not a bloody word about how we're supposed to treat the Earth. And we won't have each other without an Earth. It must be up there still. Find that other tablet.
—David Brower

Human beings have broken out of the circle of life, driven not by biological need, but by the social organization which they have devised to 'conquer' nature: means of gaining wealth that are governed by requirements conflicting with those which govern nature. The end result is the environmental crisis, a crisis of survival. Once more, to survive, we must close the circle. We must learn how to restore to nature the wealth that we borrow from it.
—Barry Commoner

Before I flew I was already aware of how small and vulnerable our planet is; but only when I saw it from space, in all its ineffable beauty and fragility, did I realize that humankind's most urgent task is to cherish and preserve it for future generations.
—Vladimir Shatalov, USSR space explorer

Notes:

TEACHING AND LEARNING

Teaching And Learning...

It seems Mother Nature is a most excellent teacher in all her splendor and beauty. I will miss my new found home, the woods.
—19 year old Outward Bound student

WHY TEACH ABOUT THE ENVIRONMENT?

Take a moment and think about why teaching about the environment is important. We all live in two worlds, the world of nature and the civilized world. Over time, most of us have lost touch with the world of nature. Our lives have become increasingly anthropocentric, or human-centered. But we remain part of a nature-centered, or ecocentric, universe whether we recognize it or not. Perhaps the primary reason we need to teach about the environment is to communicate our debt to, and our connections with, the natural world.

The natural world is our basic source of information, our primary database, or as David Brower says, "Nature is the ultimate encyclopedia." When we are awake to the natural world, then its complexity, diversity, and subtlety engage our senses to the highest degree. Nature is the best classroom for learning to see, hear, touch, smell, and taste more fully. Sharpened senses heighten our powers of observation and awareness and form a fertile ground for learning.

We teach about the natural world because it provides us with a wide range of challenging and rewarding physical and emotional experiences. Feeling at home in nature, moving around and exercising in it, learning about it with our hands and feet and scraped knees, laughing in it and enjoying it, attuning with it, feeling its inspiration, feeling empowered and renewed by it—these are the experiential reasons for teaching about the environment. As many quotes in this book attest, nature has been a primary and vital source of enjoyment, renewal, and inspiration. Those experiences are available to everyone, and while they can't be taught, teachers can help provide the atmosphere in which they are discovered.

We teach about the natural world because learning about it is important to our survival. In the first place the natural world can be dangerous. Students need to know that nature was once more perilous than it is now; they should understand the history of the partial domestication of the planet; and they should recognize what has been lost and what has been gained in the process. To raise their odds of survival, students need to recognize that the natural world is still hazardous—due to lack of experience, many think of the outdoors as just more television or as a kind of global theme park. All students need a healthy respect for the damage nature can do. (And outdoor learning needs an appropriate level of safety preparation.) But we teach about survival in a larger sense as well. Students need to be aware that the world of nature is our lifeline. We participate in and are part of the ecosystem and its cycles. Our lives, livelihoods, and qualities of life depend upon the continuing renewal of the world's resources. Students need to learn about the environment so that they can be intelligent participants in the most important debate of our time—how we balance human needs and desires with the finite resources and qualities of the natural world.

We teach about the environment because humans pose a threat to the natural world. We need to know how nature works and what we're doing wrong so that we can learn about ways to change our actions and activities. Students need to learn how they can avoid abusing the Earth personally—personal action means changes in lifestyle, changes in consumption, changes in the ways we spend our time. We also have the opportunity to teach about, to participate in, and to lead activities that help to heal the planet.

We teach about the environment to give our students more of a sense of the ecocentric as opposed to the anthropocentric. Our anthropocentrism has been responsible for much of the destruction of the world's resources. But rather than criticizing that part of ourselves which is human-centered, we should recognize that the ability to think beyond ourselves, to see our species as part of the larger web, is amazing, perhaps unique. By nurturing this perspective, we can create a healthier environment for all of nature, including ourselves.

Contrary to the accusations of some anti-environmentalists, ecocentric does not mean the worship of nature; it does not mean we should stop using nature's resources—that would be impossible—nor does it mean that the mosquito is our superior. An ecocentric perspective does mean that we recognize that all life is connected and that human life on earth is made possible by and supported by many other life forms which need our support in kind; and not only do those other forms of life need our support—they merit our respect; and not only do they merit our respect—they deserve our reverence. "I cannot but have reverence for all that is called life." That was the vision and challenge Albert Schweitzer gave us. We must avoid thinking of human needs greedily, self-indulgently, or with a sense of superiority. Rather we should think of our needs and desires from the point of view of the whole system.

Finally, we teach about the environment because it provides us, as instructors, the same experiences it provides our students. In the world of nature, there is always more to see, more to learn, more to feel. As we provide the arena for perception, observation, awareness, enjoyment, appreciation, concern, and inspiration, we have the opportunity to participate, to engage ourselves as well as our students, to learn as we teach.

> Therefore am I still
> A lover of the meadows and the woods,
> And mountains; and of all that we behold
> From this green earth; of all the mighty world
> Of eye and ear,—both what they half create,
> And what perceive; well pleased to recognize
> In nature and the language of the sense,
> The anchor of my purest thoughts, the nurse,
> The guide, the guardian of my heart, and soul
> Of all my moral being.
> —William Wordsworth

How To Teach About
The Environment

1. **Make Connections:**

a. <u>Whatever the subject, attempt to incorporate the natural world into it.</u>
Literature, science, and other subjects can include nature writing (many
examples are included in the EARTHBOOK). History and geography can
include a history of nature. Science can easily be connected, or re-con-
nected, to nature. The goal is to use texts, examples, and an approach
that includes the ecocentric as well as the anthropocentric.

> "Use normal assignments with an oudoor slant. Assign stories in read-
> ing that have a natural history basis. Calculate board feet in math,
> study local topographic maps in geography. Cook wild foods in home
> economics, make bird feeders in industrial arts. Use music class to
> explore natural sounds. Look at paintings and photos of wild areas in
> art. Use films, filmstrips, slides and all the normal teaching acces-
> sories. Just look for a nature angle."
> —Michael Link

b. <u>Always seek to make connections between the natural world and the
human-made world and between the natural world and the individual.</u>
Students (and teachers) need to be reminded where things come from—
the food on our plates didn't merely come from a can; the clothes we
wear weren't spontaneously generated at the mall; the book we read
didn't just come from the store, or even the printer. Our lives are inter-
twined with the natural world, and if we take that for granted, we will do
so at the expense of both the natural world and ourselves.

> "I often wonder how many of our children, when reaching for a loaf of
> bread see a wheat field, or taking an apple from a shelf, see a tree, or
> when eating a hamburger, know that an animal had to die to give them
> its flesh. I wonder how many know that if it weren't for the earth, no
> life as we know it could exist."
> —Tom Brown, Jr

2. "<u>Do what you can with what you have where you are</u>."
   —Theodore Roosevelt
a. <u>Get your students outdoors when you can.</u> Awakening and attunement come in part through immersion in the natural world.
b. <u>Providing awakening and attunement on a school campus, especially indoors, is more difficult.</u> Wilderness is best, but forest is great, park is good, playground is okay. Classroom will do.

> "Usually one need go no further than the backyard, school yard, or nearby open areas. There are two reasons for encouraging such proximity: minimal cost and complication of travel arrangements, and the message to children that nature explorations can and should happen right outside their own back doors."
> —Michael Link

3. **Be inspired**. Read about, think about, get out in and enjoy nature. Its variety and the capacity to learn from it are inexhaustible. Discover your own connections with the natural world. Seek joy, renewal, enthusiasm.

> "Those who dwell...among the beauties and the mysteries of the earth are never alone or weary of life...Those who contemplate the beauty of the earth find reserves of strength that will endure as long as life lasts."   —Rachel Carson

4. **Share yourself**. Try to reach your students with your enthusiasm and sincerity.

> "To communicate wonder, we must have a spirit of wonder. A leader who's filled with wonder, joy, and love for the natural world draws these good feelings out of others."
> —Joseph Cornell

5. **Remember the ecocentric**. Enough of our learning and thinking is human-centered. Whether the goal is perception, learning, enjoyment, inspiration, or diagnosis and cure, the overriding goal should be participating in an ecocentric relationship with the natural world. Avoid anthropomorphism (giving human qualities to non-human subjects).

> "The Sioux talked of 'the sacred hoop of the nation.' While they did not know the chemistry, biology, and hydraulics of the ecosystem, they seemed to sense the indivisible quality of all life. 'Everything the power of the world does is done in a circle.' 'With all beings and all things we shall be as relatives.'"
> —William O. Douglas

6. **Believe in your students, and yourself**. The great nature educators remind us that we cannot teach love for the environment. We can try to provide an atmosphere that awakens love in our students. Awakening and attunement are lifelong processes, so that in every learning situation, the teacher is also a student.

Since we can only provide an atmosphere for deeper learning on the part of students, we should teach with energy and detachment.

Even if it seems you are not reaching your students, you may be planting seeds that will come to fruition later. Believe that every student can be touched. Believe that the interaction between each person and the natural world has the potential to provide a unique relationship that will be of benefit to both, and to all.

Remember, too, that you may be the only or best link between each student and the natural world. A student's concept of the outdoors, its safety, its beauty, its vitality, its importance, can be changed by the actions of one teacher.

> "I and mine do not convince by arguments, similes, rhymes;
> We convince by our presence."
> —Walt Whitman

7. **Keep a light touch**. Remember humor, remember to smile and enjoy yourself. Remember that if the students are enjoying themselves you have in part succeeded. Remember not to be too attached to results you want to achieve. Give the results the opportunity to achieve themselves.

> "One lesson, Nature, let me learn of thee...
> Of toil unsevered from tranquillity
> Too great for haste, too high for rivalry."
> —Matthew Arnold

8. Be Careful with Facts

a. <u>You don't necessarily have to know facts</u>...

> "Knowing the names that humans have given to other creatures or things is far from the most important lesson you will teach. If a child asked me a question that suggested even a faint awareness of the mystery behind the arrival of a migrant sandpiper on the beach of an August morning, I would be far more pleased than by the mere fact that he knew it was a sandpiper and not a plover."
> —Rachel Carson

> "Don't feel badly about not knowing names. The names of plants and animals are only superficial labels for what those things really are."
> —Joseph Cornell

b. ...<u>but knowing the facts helps</u>... The facts you know may open up worlds for your students, especially when your outlook has an ecocentric foundation. While environmental literature offers many statements that tell us why we shouldn't teach the names of things, and while such assertions make a compelling case, it should be remembered that many of our great nature writers are also naturalists and not only know the names but use them for significant ends. Thoreau, Muir, and Burroughs, Rachel Carson, Tom Brown Jr., and Joseph Cornell love the world in part by their specific understanding of it. At the very least there are some students who will be helped and inspired by knowing the names as well as by the sense of wonder and mystery.

> "Whenever you have learned to discriminate the birds, or the plants, or the geological features of a country, it is as if new and keener eyes were added."
> —John Burroughs

c. <u>...but remember that words can get in the way</u>. Too often we assume that the word is the thing. Many of nature's lessons can be taught without words.

> "What's in a name? White Oak, *Quercus alba*: does the name tell us of the five foods and five medications that come from the tree? Does the name tell us the color of the flames when burned, the scent of the smoke, the color the smoke gives to our buckskins, or the unique taste it gives to our cooked foods? Does the name tell of the dyes and glues that can be gleaned from the acorns and inner bark, or does it tell what animals feed upon it or find shelter in its branches? Of course not, yet most people are content knowing only the name."
> —Tom Brown, Jr.

9. <u>**Treat nature with respect**</u>. Don't trap, kill, abuse, pick, plunder, or disturb. Look for alternatives to bringing nature indoors.

> "For my own part I seldom take rocks home, no matter where I might find them; in my opinion they are best enjoyed in situ, where God Himself, so to speak, and the leisurely economy of Nature have seen fit to deposit them."
> —Edward Abbey

10. <u>**Keep it active**</u>. The best learning engages students' bodies and senses as well as their minds. Learning by doing, learning that includes visual or tactile stimulation, and learning with movement echo the flow and activity of nature. Remember art as well and the opportunity for creativity involving nature or a nature theme.

> "Remember: in our work it is not show and tell, but share and do."
> —Steve van Matre

11. <u>**Offer positive messages about the environment**</u>. Whether outdoors or indoors, whatever the activity, give your students positive messages about the environment. Negative messages are everywhere. The weatherperson tells us that rainy days are horrible, a hot day intolerable, a cold

day nearly unendurable. The media and many other sources communicate that bugs are gross, garbage is nasty, and dirt is bad. It is up to those of us who know better to communicate pleasure in the natural world as it is and relate the importance of every phase and part of nature.

"A rainy day is the perfect time for a walk in the woods."
—Rachel Carson

"Let me go wheree'er I will,
I hear a sky-born music still:
It sounds from all things old,
It sounds from all things young,
From all that's fair, from all that's foul,
Peals out a cheerful song.
It is not only in the rose,
It is not only in the bird,
Not only where the rainbow glows,
Nor in the song of woman heard,
But in the darkest, meanest things
There alway, alway something sings.
...T' is not in the high stars alone,
Nor in the cups of budding flowers,
Nor in the red-breast's mellow tone,
Nor in the bow that smiles in showers,
But in the mud and scum of things
There alway, alway something sings."
—Ralph Waldo Emerson

---

12. **Define your terms**. Many assumptions are inherent in the words we use and students need to confront the implications of words and their definitions. We throw things "away" as though away were a place, when actually we are throwing them into our own environment. A "sanitary landfill" is sanitary is one sense but not in others. "Environmentally friendly" packaging may be, but then again it may not. "Recycled paper" may have 10% pre-consumer material in it or it may be 100% post-consumer (The paper in this book is 100% recycled and 50% post-consumer). What does "recycling" really mean? In what sense are some forms of life "above" or "higher" than others. More about the use of words can be found in the section "Working with Words."

Problems With Teaching About The Environment

1. <u>As an educator you are charged with teaching your students to think. As an environmentalist you are charged with sharing your inspirations, opinions, and concerns. How do you stay fair to both your students and your values?</u>

   Teach inspiration, celebration and appreciation of nature first. An ecocentric perspective is the most important environmental lesson you can share. When it comes to teaching specific issues, many environmental educators recommend presenting major sides of the issues, allowing your students to make up their minds, and only then expressing your opinion for them to put into perspective. If a view opposed to your own is expressed, give it a fair hearing; don't use your position of authority to suppress the flow of ideas.

2. <u>Ecology is a relatively young science. How do you know that your facts are right?</u>

   In some cases you don't. In some cases today's "fact" might be tomorrow's "fiction" (and possibly day after tomorrow's fact again). You and your students need to learn to remain flexible in face of changing information. Communicate the need for that flexibility. Remember to provide the sources of your information to help establish the perspective from which the information comes.

   There are some issues about which we may never know the facts, which is another reason to cultivate an ecocentric perspective; then if we err, at least we err on the side of nature. In *The House of Life*, writing about Rachel Carson's position on pesticides, Paul Brooks says that her basic argument was "that we simply do not have enough scientific knowledge to assess accurately the risks we run when we use these poisons, and that they should be certified for safety before their first use." Brooks continues: "The chemical industry, of course, had taken the opposite view: that it is all right to use them unless the danger has been proved beyond reasonable doubt. **This conflict of philosophies**—which is not confined to pesticides—**remains one of the basic conflicts of our time.**" (Emphasis added)

   And in *Environmental Science*, Nebel and Wright consider the question of Cornucopians (those who assume that Earth's bounty is virtually unending and/or that technology will save us from any fix we get ourselves into) and Conservationists.

They conclude:

> "Who is right? Time will tell. Yes, but this is not like a sporting event that you can watch and then go home to life as usual. If we place our bets with the Cornucopians and lose, we lose the world. If we place our bets with the environmentalists and achieve a sustainable society, the most we can lose is to never know whether the Cornucopians were right or wrong."

3. <u>You have come across environmental education materials, produced by corporations, which downplay environmental problems. How should you respond to those materials?</u>

Corporate awareness of environmental issues continues to evolve. Many businesses have discovered that it isn't very expensive to become better environmental citizens. Others have recognized that they can save or even make money by developing technologies that save or renew resources. Environmentalists need to recognize that corporations will be, in fact must be, participants in solving environmental problems.

Also, there is honest disagreement about environmental issues among conservationists, businesspeople, and citizens. Remember that the majority of people, whatever their ecological perspective, are well-meaning and sincere; there are many differing points of view held by people who consider themselves conservationists; there is plenty of room for honest disagreement about environmental problems and solutions. There are also people on both sides of environmental issues who distort the issues, sometimes from lack of knowledge, often because they have such an unshakable faith in their own points of view that they can't see any alternatives. Three of the major distortions—oversimplification, dogmatism, and self-righteousness—are discussed in the next section.

Corporate sponsored environmental materials will try to reflect well on the efforts of the sponsoring corporation. In some cases the results can be closer to indoctrination than education. One guide, for example, argues that disposable diapers are as environmentally sound as cloth diapers (The corporation happens to manufacture disposable diapers.). The guide also says that clearcutting forests creates new habitat for wildlife and that there is no alternative to the use of CFC's; these claims are just plain wrong (Clearcutting is a significant destroyer of wildlife habitat, and CFC's are being successfully phased out.).

While virtually all environmental materials will contain information that is open to question, the instructor must decide whether or not misinformation is an intentional distortion. And if the distortion is intentional, the teacher must decide if that's part of the lesson she wants to share with her students.

Be aware, too, that there is a strong, well-funded anti-environmental movement, which intentionally distorts facts, attacks the character and motives of environmentalists, creates fake organizations that sound ecological but aren't, produces slanted surveys and studies, and tries to tell the public that there really isn't much to be concerned about. E.O. Wilson, two-time Pulitzer Prize winner and renowned biologist and author, recently noted that the major problem facing conservation is not public apathy but "the determined efforts of the anti-environmentalists who are trying to change public opinion." When asked how one should deal with anti-environmentalists, E.O. Wilson said, "Educate, educate, educate. Keep talking, keep pointing out, keep explaining, keep demonstrating—show the wonderful beauty and promise of the natural world."

For more information on the anti-environmental movement see *The Greenpeace Guide to Anti-Environmental Organizations.*

4. <u>You sometimes despair when you think about the extent of the environmental problems we face. What should you do?</u>

Sorrow, frustration, and doubt are appropriate responses to the environmental crisis—so are hope and action—so is joy in the world we have. If you are a teacher by profession, you have the opportunity to reach many students each year, year after year. If you aren't a teacher by profession, you can still teach about the environment. Even the teachers are learners; even the learners are teachers.

THREE PITFALLS TO AVOID

Both Environmentalists and Cornucopians can and do make mistakes; so do instructors. Three pitfalls especially worth noting are Oversimplification, Dogmatism, and Self-Righteousness. Each of these will be addressed separately, though as the examples will show, they overlap.

Oversimplification. Offering simple answers to complex issues both trivializes the issues and hurts environmental understanding.

For example, an environmentalist who says that one ounce of concentrated dioxin can kill a million people is guilty of oversimplification. What makes that statement a figure of speech rather than a statistic is the fact that nothing could deliver that concentrated ounce to that million or more people. If gun control advocates argued that one handgun could kill a million or more people, they might be correct theoretically, but they wouldn't have a cogent gun-control argument. This type of oversimplification ultimately hurts the environment by hurting the credibility of its advocates.

On the other hand, arguments by, for example, the pulpwood industry that they have preserved the environment by planting more trees than they have cut is also oversimplification. Trees do not make a forest or an ecosystem. Monoculture tree farms threaten species and destroy biodiversity. To act as if they replicate natural processes is an oversimplification.

Dogmatism. We don't know all of the answers and shouldn't pretend to. There are those who contend that: human needs always take precedence over the needs of other creatures; that wild is always better than civilized; that civilized is always better than wild; that pesticides are always bad; that pesticides pose no threat; that clearcuts should never be allowed; that clearcuts are the way to handle forests.

Then there are various theories, including the Greenhouse Effect and the effects of CFC's on the global environment. The truth is, ultimately, that no one knows exactly what's going to happen. The range of scientific predictions should convince us that we are not dealing with certainties. If someone "knows" that Miami will sink or if someone "knows" that there will be no climactic changes, they are being dogmatic rather than informative.

There are those who state with dogmatic assurance that we have no environmental problems. Among those who acknowledge problems there are those who have "the solution" for various environmental ills. But the attempt to solve large problems is usually far from simple. For example, the fast-food industry originally moved to plastic packaging in part because environmentalists insisted that paper packaging wasted too many resources—in that case the cure may have been worse than the disease. In 1990, recycling was touted by many as "the" solution to our waste problems; when inevitable problems arose, people were disillusioned.

All of us are capable of making mistakes and have plenty to learn. We have to remain flexible in the face of changing information and technologies. When we choose "solutions" to environmental problems, we should recognize that we are choosing to face new and different kinds of problems. We should recognize that much about natural processes is not yet understood. Most importantly, we have to remember to let our flexibility and problem-solving be guided by a commitment to and concern for the whole planet.

Self-righteousness. Moral judgments are counterproductive. Environmentalists need to recognize that the environment is not an us-versus-them issue. There is no "them." There is only "us." We all need to learn; we all participate in the destruction of the environment; none of us is in a position to feel or act superior. Even if the opposition is acting out of self-interest, manipulatively, or dishonestly, we have to assume that their basic problem is lack of understanding.

In writing about ozone depletion a conservationist author asked how it could be that we created a situation where we were threatening life on the planet for the sake of aerosol spray. The author's answer: "Profits, as always, overruled common sense..." Such an attitude is incorrect (we had no way of knowing that CFC's would destroy the ozone layer) and self-righteous; as such it fails to accomplish its goal of adequately educating either users of CFC's or the public. Another form of self-righteousness involves criticizing others for their environmental errors without putting our own into perspective. In his essay "Forerunners of Environmental Education," Malcolm Swan offers some much-needed perspective:

"The disregard for the environment attributed to this nation's builders is difficult for most people to comprehend. Historical accounts show them almost as barbarians, moving across the continent in an orgy of death and destruction. With no regard for anything not a product of human hands, so the accounts go, they set forth to subdue the wilderness...

"The mentality that led to all of this, however, may have been no different from the mentality of the mid-20th century which permitted the air, water, countryside, and seas to be used as common cesspools in which to spew forth the wastes of our time—all this in spite of conservationism having originated some decades earlier. Nor is it greatly different from the mid-70's thinking that calls for the daily combustion of billions of gallons of petroleum—a resource much too precious to be depleted as fuel if one has any regard for unborn generations. In the long run, the Virginia planter who injured his land by growing cotton or tobacco may have been no more guilty than his modern counterpart who constructs wide strips of concrete across the fertile soils of northern Illinois. In the eyes of history, the results are apt to be much the same."

Konrad Lorenz adds this thought: "If the great errors of our Western civilization are usually first committed in America, it is also the country in which these errors are first recognized and corrected."

Self-righteousness and dogmatism also contribute to an authoritarian preachiness that may be conducive to indoctrination but is not conducive to education. What is needed for education is genuine enthusiasm, flexibility, a degree of detachment, and a healthy dose of curiosity.

Learning To See

In the 1960's Marshall McLuhan wrote about media and their effects on human beings. He contended that our technologies affect how we use our senses and the balance of the senses. Books created an eye-oriented culture, one where people relied more on sight at the expense of other senses, and one in which eyes were used most often to focus on specific items, such as the text of a book.

The Balance of the Senses: McLuhan asked the reader to imagine walking a plank one foot wide and six inches from the ground—obviously it is an easy thing to do. Then he asks us to imagine walking that same plank 100 feet from the ground. Now walking the plank is almost impossible. McLuhan says that the fear is much worse for members of "the Gutenberg galaxy" because of the eye-orientation of our senses. Navajo Indians were hired to build skyscrapers in early New York because they weren't as afraid of heights, and McLuhan claims that they weren't as afraid of heights because they came from an aural rather than a visual culture. One way to bring the other senses more into focus is with blindfold activities, several of which are contained in this book. Other specific exercises that emphasize hearing, touch, taste, and smell also help. Students can experiment, in "One Square Foot," "Green Spot," and other activities with changing the focus of their sensory awareness.

McLuhan also says that altering our senses can lead us to alter our perspectives of the world. A sight-based, print-oriented culture, he said, tends toward regimentation and specialization; nature becomes something to be organized and manipulated. This may be one reason why blindfold and other sense-focusing activities are such good learning tools.

Wide-Angle Vision: Tom Brown, Jr. refers to our focused vision as "tunneling vision" and offers "wide-angle, or full peripheral vision" as an alternative. We use wide-angle vision 1% of the time, Brown says, but should attempt to use it 50% of the time. To use it, he recommends "pretending the whole scene" around you "is a picture hanging on the wall...Observe the landscape in its entirety, pushing the frame as far out" as possible. The viewer will automatically "start picking up movement and begin to sense things on a broader level." More on wide-angle and other types of vision are in *Tom Brown's Field Guide to Nature and Survival for Children*.

Some persons seem to have opened more eyes than others, they see with such force and distinctness; their vision penetrates the tangle and obscurity where that of others fails...

How many eyes did...Thoreau open? how many did Audubon? Not outward eyes, but inward. We open another eye whenever we see beyond the first general features or outlines of things—whenever we grasp the special details and characteristic markings that this mask covers. Science confers new powers of vision. Whenever you have learned to discriminate the birds, or the plants, or the geological features of a country, it is as if new and keener eyes were added.
—John Burroughs

Night Vision: Edward Abbey, out at night with a flashlight, recognized the importance of not using it: "The flashlight...is a useful instrument in certain situations but I can see the road well enough without it. Better, in fact. There's another disadvantage to the use of the flashlight: like many other mechanical gadgets it tends to separate a man from the world around him. If I switch it on my eyes adapt to it and I can see only the small pool of light which it makes in front of me; I am isolated. Leaving the flashlight in my pocket where it belongs, I remain a part of the environment I walk through and my vision though limited has no sharp or definite boundary." Note: Remember on your night outings to spend time without the flashlight. After turning flashlights off, it sometimes takes half an hour or longer for the eyes to fully adjust to the darkness.

Silent Hike: The idea here is to move as silently as possible, engaging all of the senses. No one should talk. The instructor, if knowledgeable enough, could introduce things to taste and to smell. At times some senses could be shut out with blindfolds or earplugs or mittens to sharpen other senses.

We should take children into nature frequently so the senses are fed, nurtured, and become keen. We should set an example, by pointing out subtle sounds, sights, smells, tastes, and feelings. Only through our careful attention and nurturing will children ever hope to reach their full sensory potential. Keen sensory awareness is one of the most important skills children can have in life, and it is sensory awareness that makes life rich and full.
　　　　　　　—Tom Brown, Jr.

All one to me—sandstorm or sunshine I am content, so long as I have something to eat, good health, the earth to take my stand on, and light behind the eyes to see by.
　　　　　　　—Edward Abbey

Camera: Joseph Cornell also promotes the use of blindfold activities. One of his best, found in *Sharing the Joy of Nature*, is "Camera." One person is the photographer, the other the camera. In this variation the camera does not wear a blindfold; she simply keeps her eyes closed. The photographer guides the camera, sets up the shots, "presses the shutter button by tapping the camera's shoulder;" the camera opens her eyes to see the scene that has been set up for her; when tapped again, she closes her eyes. The photographer moves the camera from scene to scene. Then they change roles.

Find the Difference: Students study a small natural area then close their eyes while the instructor or another student changes something about the area. Then the students open their eyes and try to identify what is different.

Working With Words

Words are tools that can be used well or poorly, to reveal or to hide, to clarify or to distort. We sometimes fall into word traps, such as: (1) thinking about something differently because of the words associated with it, (2) taking a thing for granted because of its label, (3) using words without having clearly defined their meanings, (4) using words that reflect a bias without perceiving that bias, and (5) identifying words too closely with things. Here are examples of each of these traps as they relate to environmental education.

(1) **How about Father Nature**?: When we refer to Nature as a "she" or as "Mother Nature," does that make it easier for us to take advantage of "her?" Aren't mothers considered more giving, more sacrificing, and more exploitable than fathers? What if in the course of environmental education we took a few weeks and referred to nature as "Father Nature" or as "he?" What if we assumed that if we didn't behave, that if we abused "Father Nature" too much, that we would be chastised or punished by his power. Or what if we referred to it as "Baby Nature," a helpless lovely jewel in need of our care and nurturing? Each term says something about Nature's qualities, and each contains unhealthy stereotypes. Unless we're willing to treat "Mother Nature" with more respect, it may be time to depersonify Nature altogether.

"Natural resources" seem "exploitable." What if we called potentially exploitable nature "Natural Qualities," or "Natural Treasures"?

Think of other environmental terms that would be thought of differently if their names were changed.

(2) **Have you ever seen a squirrel**?: What do see when you think of a squirrel? Do you see a versatile, quick, graceful mammal with sharp claws that allow it to dance up, down, and around the surfaces of trees? Or do you see a frightened blur dodging its way across a street? Do you see a miracle or just an animate object? Do you see an individual squirrel with its own personality or do you assume, either verbally or nonverbally, that if you've seen one squirrel you've seen them all?

Do you think squirrels are interesting? Have you spent much time watching them? What if you observed the lives of squirrels in your neighborhood and described them in writing but did not use the word "squirrel." What if, instead, you described the highly mobile, intelligent, nest-building mammal "rersquil"? What if the neighborhood alley cat was the exotic predatory mammal "lacletay"? Consider making such an assignment to students. They can create a name for a commonly seen animal, make up a new name for it, and describe its abilities and habits with wonder. There is no "just a squirrel." There probably is no "just a" anything.

(3) **If a tree fell in the forest and nobody was there, would it be recycled**?: What is "recycling"? Is it the manufacturing process that takes place after collecting and processing materials? Or does it include collecting materials at curbside? Or might it also be shorthand for the entire environmental processes of reducing, reusing, recycling, and composting? Does it include natural processes of decay and regeneration? The definition depends on who you ask.

"Resource recovery" should be a synonym for the process of recycling but has been adopted by the incineration industry.

To some people "forest" is trees and to others "forest" is an ecosystem.

Is "environmental education" education that takes place outdoors, education that teaches conservation, education that teaches about nature, education that teaches appreciation of nature, education that teaches about environmental problems, education that relates the environment to all other subjects? It depends on who's talking.

The use of buzz words or words with multiple meanings creates interesting discussions. Other such words and terms include "solid waste," "sanitary landfill," "wise use," "throw away."

(4) **Read any groundbreaking environmental books lately**?: Some of the words we use presume that human activities take precedence over natural activities. "Groundbreaking," for example, which means innovative, implies that cultivation of the Earth is a significant improvement over natural processes. A "cultivated" person is considered a superior person because cultivated land is considered superior property. Looking at the roots of words can help students understand them better. "Cultivated" is definitely agricultural. "Jungle" comes from wasteland or desert. "Savage" comes from a root meaning "woods." "Primitive," which has both positive and negative meanings, comes from a root word meaning "first." "Waste" comes from a Latin verb meaning "to make empty," while "nature" comes from "to be born." Which of these have negative, positive, or neutral connotations?

Some terminology was invented, sometimes for reasons that have more to do with public relations than accuracy. A "sanitary landfill" is far from sanitary. "Even-aged harvest" is a nice way of saying "clearcutting." "Bycatch waste" consists of living aquatic creatures killed in the process of "harvesting" other aquatic creatures for food (Dolphins killed while catching tuna, or the 90% of a shrimp fisherman's catch that isn't shrimp, are "bycatch waste."). "Low-level" radioactive waste encompasses radiation readings from minor to deadly. A nuclear accident is an "incident" and an explosion in a nuclear power plant might be called an "energetic disassembly."

Students can make up their own definitions to counter the intrinsic or invented propaganda in words. A weed, which is defined as an undesirable or unproductive plant, can also be defined as "a plant whose benefit to people has not yet been discovered," or "a necessary part of the biosphere that humans haven't figured out how to exploit." What is a pest? Maybe it's "a vital part of the ecosystem which irritates or competes with humans." What are "consumer goods" and how "good" are they? Doesn't the term "natural resource" imply something intended for exploitation? What are "garbage," "trash," "rubbish," "refuse"? What is a "waste product"?

(5). **A rose is a rose is no rose**: Encourage students to recognize that the thing is not the word, that the word is only a label of convenience, that a "tree" isn't really a "tree"; rather it is something we choose, or chose, to give the name "tree" to.

Silence in a natural setting can do more than inspire contemplation. It can inspire a break from the incessant flow of words that generally travel through our brains. To sit quietly in the world of nature and to see things while trying not to attach words to them, and to see them less as things and more as interactions with one another, offers an important mental and emotional change of pace from the our usual word-dominated way of looking at the world.

"You want those sodas in a "Organic Farmers Do It Better" glass.
a "I ♥ Dolphin Free Tuna Fish" cup or a "Have You Hugged A Tree Today" mug?"

John Heine

Readings: Teaching And Learning

One stormy autumn night when my nephew Roger was about twenty months old I wrapped him in a blanket and carried him down to the beach in the rainy darkness. Out there, just at the edge of where-we-couldn't-see, big waves were thundering in, dimly seen white shapes that boomed and shouted and threw great handfuls of froth at us. Together we laughed for pure joy—he a baby meeting for the first time the wild tumult of Oceanus, I with the salt of half a lifetime of sea love in me. But I think we felt the same spine-tingling response to the vast, roaring ocean and the wild night around us.

—Rachel Carson

In environmental affairs we should primarily try to influence people toward beautiful acts by finding ways to work on their inclinations rather than their morals. Unhappily, the extensive moralizing within the ecological movement has given the public the false impression that they are primarily asked to sacrifice, to show more responsibility, more concern, and better morals. As I see it we need the immense variety of sources of joy opened through increased sensitivity toward the richness and diversity of life, through the profound cherishing of free natural landscapes... The requisite care flows naturally if the self is widened and deepened so that protection of free nature is felt and conceived of as protection of our very selves.

—Arne Naess

Take long walks in stormy weather or through deep snow in the fields and woods, if you would keep your spirits up. Deal with brute nature. Be cold and hungry and weary.

—Henry David Thoreau

Even when I was wet, exhausted, and ached all over, I felt terrific.
—48 year old Outward Bound student

A venturesome minority will always be eager to set off on their own, and no obstacles should be placed in their path; let them take risks, for Godsake, let them get lost, sunburnt, stranded, drowned, eaten by bears, buried alive under avalanches—that is the right and privilege of any free American. But the rest, the majority, most of them new to the out-of-doors, will need and welcome assistance, instruction, and guidance. Many will not know how to saddle a horse, read a topographical map, follow a trail over

slickrock, memorize landmarks, build a fire in rain, treat snakebite, rappel down a cliff, glissade down a glacier, read a compass, find water under sand, load a burro, splint a broken bone, bury a body, patch a rubber boat, portage a waterfall, survive a blizzard, avoid lightning, cook a porcupine, comfort a girl during a thunderstorm, predict the weather, dodge falling rock, climb out of a box canyon...
                         —Edward Abbey

Of all the things that might be true about experiential education, the one thing that is unassailably true is that you can't find out by defining it.
                         —John Huie

In terms of the true meaning of Outward Bound, I picked up one answer why I came: compassion. Compassion for those less capable than myself. Compassion for my fellows. And compassion for the glorious woods, mountains, and rivers God has given us, and thankful for those with the passion to work to protect them.
                         —35 year old Outward Bound student.

The mode of founding a college is, commonly, to get up a subscription of dollars and cents, and then following blindly the principles of a division of labor to its extreme, a principle which should never be followed but with circumspection,—to call in a contractor who makes this a subject of speculation, and he employs Irishmen or other operatives actually to lay the foundations, while the students that are to be are said to be fitting themselves for it; and for these oversights successive generations have to pay.

I think that it would be better that this, for the students, or those who desire to be benefited by it, even to lay the foundation themselves. The student who secures his coveted leisure and retirement by systematically shirking any labor necessary to man obtains but an ignoble and unprofitable leisure, defrauding himself of the experience which alone can make leisure fruitful.

"But," says one, "you do not mean that the students should go to work with their hands instead of their heads?" I do not mean that exactly, but I mean something which he might think a good deal like that; I mean that they should not play life, or study it merely, while the community supports them at this expensive game, but earnestly live it from beginning to end.

How could youths better learn to live than by at once trying the experiment of living? Methinks this would exercise their minds as much as mathematics. If I wished a boy to know something about the arts and sciences, for instance, I would not pursue the common course, which is merely to send him into the neighborhood of some professor, where any thing is professed and practiced but the art of life;—to survey the world through a telescope or a microscope, and never with his natural eye; to study chemistry, and not learn how his bread is made, or mechanics, and not learn how it is earned; to discover new satellites to Neptune, and not detect the motes in his eyes, or to what vagabond he is a satellite himself; or to be devoured by the monsters that swarm all around him, while contemplating the monsters in a drop of vinegar.

Which would have advanced the most at the end of a month,—the boy who had made his own jackknife from the ore which he had dug and smelted, reading as much as would be necessary for this,—or the boy who had attended the lectures on metallurgy at the Institute in the mean while, and had received a Rogers' penknife from his father? Which would be most likely to cut his fingers?...

To my astonishment I was informed on leaving college that I had studied navigation! —why, if I had taken one turn down the harbor I should have known more about it.

Even the poor student studies and is taught only political economy, while that economy of living which is synonymous with philosophy is not even sincerely professed in our colleges. The consequence is, that while he is reading Adam Smith, Ricardo, and Say, he runs his father in debt irretrievably.

—Henry David Thoreau in *Walden*
(all originally one paragraph)

John Heine

BACKPAGES

Outward Bound:
An Introduction

I regard it as the foremost task of education to insure the survival of these qualities: an enterprising curiosity, an undefeatable spirit, tenacity in pursuit, readiness for sensible self-denial and, above all, compassion.
— Kurt Hahn, founder of Outward Bound.

The first Outward Bound School was established by Kurt Hahn in Great Britain in 1941. Hahn had escaped to Britain from Nazi Germany in the 1930's; soon after he founded The Gordonstoun School in Wales, which sought to teach strength of character and responsible citizenship as well as academics.

In the early years of the Second World War, Germany attacked and sunk many British merchant ships. British officials noted with alarm that younger, presumably stronger sailors were dying at sea while their older companions were surviving. Hahn believed that the young sailors simply had not developed the fortitude, self-reliance, and confidence that the older sailors had acquired through experience. Hahn designed a program to instill in these young sailors a sense of self-confidence, team loyalty, and the ability to endure life-threatening hardships. This was the first Outward Bound School.

"Outward Bound" took its name from the nautical term used when ships left the safety of the harbor and ventured into the hazards of the open sea. In an arduous 28-day program, the young seamen developed the skills they needed in order to survive under adverse conditions.

Outward Bound's approach was defined by Hahn's belief that the willingness to persevere in the face of misfortune depended more on attitude than physical strength. He incorporated this belief into tenets he designated as the four Pillars of Outward Bound: Self-reliance, Fitness, Craftsmanship, Compassion. These objectives continue to give form and meaning to Outward Bound programs worldwide.

Outward Bound is a non-profit, educational organization with a focus on experiential learning. Its international network includes nearly 50 schools on five continents. Vital components of Outward Bound courses include physical challenges (such as rock climbing, whitewater canoeing, and backpacking), teambuilding, and service projects. Courses last from a few days to several months, with most courses between 8 and 23 days.

One of the best ways to get an idea of the Outward Bound experience is to read from the writings of people who have taken courses. Quotes from Outward Bound students that relate to the environment are found throughout the EARTHBOOK. Some of the following student quotations are also environmental, while others communicate further aspects and inspirations of the Outward Bound experience.

Outward Bound has made me appreciate nature with all its fruits and thorns.
—18 year old

Outward Bound has given me a new sense of loving the outdoors and the land we live on. I want to become more conscious of our good earth and do my part to conserve and save it.
—29 year old

It has taught me how to live in Nature's world with the trees, animals, and bugs.
—14 year old

I can never go outdoors and not be able to notice what a wonderful place it is. Rain will never bother me again when I have a nice warm place to go into afterwards... Nothing I have ever done in my life so far has meant as much to me as this course has. I plan for my children to all get to come someday.
—38 year old

I pushed myself to the limit and when I got there I found that I liked who I am.
—18 year old

I wanted a physical and mental tune-up from the course and got a major overhaul.
—30 year old

Outward Bound taught me to live life, every minute, as a celebration and exclamation of life.
—20 year old

I leave with a true sense of knowing that the seemingly impossible is possible. That the 'I can't do that' is doable. That the 'I'll never make it' is makable. That the 'I can't climb that' is climbable.
—39 year old

I basically hated the course but learned so much from it I think it was worth it.
—15 year old

Half of the time we spent laughing, and the other half we could have bent over in tears. But I am satisfied with my experience and would recommend it to any masochist.
—15 year old

I haven't played as much as I have in the last three weeks for absolutely years, and it has felt wonderful. I intend to do more of it on a day to day basis.
—44 year old

Even as I fight cancer and anticipate more surgery, the role I play is the educator, encourager, and the empathizer. In recent weeks, there has been a growing doubt that I have the inner resources to live up to my expectations of me. Outward Bound seemed to be just the answer to my need, and by golly, I believe it was! Now, fired up, I promise to keep that inner fire stoked everyday and radiate the warmth and power rekindled here.
—54 year old

I can't express exactly how much it meant to me! The whole thing was incredibly HARD and though now when I think back I loved it, I can vividly remember times when I hated it with a violent passion and wanted to stop! But I feel that I succeeded and learned so much!
—15 year old

I have learned how to find that little voice inside me that says, "You can do it."
—14 year old

*I have **never** been so cold, wet, tired, frustrated, and happy in all my life.*
—28 year old

To see a 46 year old man weep in terror as he faces a rock climb, and then to see that man accomplish a 120 foot rappel the next day—with a smile on his face no less, that is the Outward Bound experience.
—37 year old

I came here a boxer. I left a dancer. In the clouds on the top of a mountain, I saw a new way.
—42 year old

The Outward Bound experience has proven to be powerful, unique, and wonderful for many people. While there are exceptions (**"These nine days** have been the most miserable I have ever spent in my life." "I felt that Outward Bound was made to look fun when it was way too intensive...Personally I recommend that nobody ever take an Outward Bound course again."), over 90% of NCOBS students surveyed within a year of their courses were overwhelmingly positive in their assessments.

Outward Bound, then, is an educational process dedicated to the principle that the individual develops self-confidence, concern for others, and self-awareness in the broad scheme of things when confronted by challenging, shared experiences involving service and adventure.

From the Outward Bound USA Mission Statement: "Outward bound is a non-profit educational organization whose primary purpose is to develop in our students respect for self, care for others, responsibility to the community and sensitivity to the environment..."

Outward Bound Trust — is the founding organization in Great Britain which operates five schools in the British Isles and charters schools throughout the world. Outward Bound UK Trust; Gulliver House; Madeira Walk; Windsor, Berks; SL4 1EU, Great Britain. Telephone (44) 1753-810-753.

Outward Bound USA — is the parent organization in the United States, chartered by the Outward Bound Trust, and consisting of a national body (OBN) and five Outward Bound Schools. Outward Bound USA; Route 9D; R2, Box 280; Garrison, NY 10524-9757. Telephone: (800) 243-8520 or (914) 424-4000.

Colorado Outward Bound School — 945 Pennsylvania Street; Denver, CO 80203. Telephone; (800) 477-2627 or (303) 837-0880.

Hurricane Island Outward Bound School — P.O. Box 429; Rockland, ME 04841. Telephone (800) 341-1744 or (207) 594-5548.

New York City Outward Bound Center; 140 West Street, Suite 2626; New York, NY 10007. Telephone (212) 608-8899

North Carolina Outward Bound School — 2582 Riceville Road; Asheville, NC 28805. Telephone (800) 841-0186 or (704) 299-3366.

Pacific Crest Outward Bound School — 0100 SW Bancroft Street; Portland, OR 97201. Telephone (800) 547- 3312 or (503) 243-1446.

Thompson Island Outward Bound Education Center: P.O. Box 127; Boston, MA 02127. Telephone (617) 328-3900.

Voyageur Outward Bound School — 111 Third Avenue South; Minneapolis, MN 55401-2551. Telephone (800) 328-2943 or (612) 338-0565.

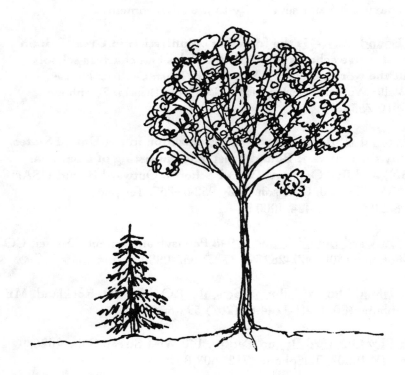

Resources...

There seems to be no end of environmental books. The list below is a bibliography of books and other materials that were either resources or inspirations for the EARTHBOOK.

A more comprehensive list of environmental books can be found in *The Environmentalist's Bookshelf: A Guide to the Best Books*, by Robert Meredith (New York: G.K. Hall & Co., 1993). Environmentalists were asked about their favorite or most influential books; the 500 top vote getters are listed and summarized. The #1 environmental book, according to this survey, is Aldo Leopold's *A Sand County Almanac and Sketches Here and There*. The rest of the top five were: Rachel Carson's *Silent Spring*; *State of the World* by Lester R. Brown and the staff of Worldwatch Institute; *The Population Bomb* by Paul R. Ehrlich; and Henry David Thoreau's *Walden*. For more details and 495 more potential books to read, see *The Environmentalist's Bookshelf*.

Note the following: Materials that are environmental, educational, and experiential are listed in boldface type.

Abbey, Edward. *Beyond the Wall: Essays from the Outside*. New York: Holt, Rinehart and Winston, 1984.
—*Desert Solitaire: A Season in the Wilderness*. New York: Simon & Schuster, 1968. Two fine efforts from the curmudgeon of environmentalism.

Alabama Environmental Council. "Landowners, Don't Miss Out." Birmingham, AL, 1994. A booklet which provides alternatives to clearcutting.

Armstrong, Virginia Irving, editor. *I Have Spoken: American History Through the Voices of the Indians*. New York: Swallow Press, 1971.

Arnold, Matthew (1822-1888). Poems.

Baker, Richard St. Barbe. *My Life, My Trees*. Forres, Scotland: Findhorn Publications, 1970. An early conservationist shares stories of his attempts at reclaiming deserts with trees and of working to save the redwoods in the United States.

Beston, Henry. *The Outermost House*. New York: Random House, 1928. "A year of life on the great beach of Cape Cod."

Black Elk. See Neihardt, John.

Brooks, Paul. *The House of Life: Rachel Carson at Work*. Boston: Houghton Mifflin Company, 1989. A fine biography with extensive selections from Carson's work.

Brown, Tom Jr. *Tom Brown's Field Guide to Nature and Survival for Children*. New York: Berkeley Books, 1989. Filled with words of inspiration and practical wisdom. The orientation is pioneer and Native American.

Brundtland Report, The. See World Commission on Environment and Development.

Burroughs, John (1837-1921). *Locusts and Wild Honey*; *Winter Sunshine*

Byron, Lord (George Gordon) (1788-1824). Poems.

Carpenter, Edward (1844-1929). Poems.

Carson, Rachel. *The Sea Around Us*. New York: Oxford University Press, 1950.
The Sense of Wonder. New York: Harper & Row, 1956.
Silent Spring. Boston: Houghton, Mifflin and Co., 1962.

Commoner, Barry. *The Closing Circle: Nature, Man, and Technology*. New York: Alfred A. Knopf, 1971. "Most of this book is an effort to discover which human acts have broken the circle of life, and why." A clear presentation of the complexity of ecology and the crises we create.

Cornell, Joseph. *Sharing Nature with Children*. Ananda Publications, 1979.
—*Listening to Nature*. Nevada City, CA: Dawn Publications, 1987.
—*Sharing the Joy of Nature*. Nevada City, CA: Dawn Publications, 1989.
These books are wonderful introductions to discovering the natural world. All three are very good, and *Sharing Nature with Children* is a classic.
Council on Environmental Quality. *Environmental Trends* (22nd Annual Report). Washington, DC, 1992. From the Executive Office of the President of the United States.

Cousteau, Jacques-Yves, and the Staff of the Cousteau Society. *The Cousteau Almanac: An Inventory of Life on Our Water Planet*. New York: Doubleday and Co., 1981.

Douglas, William O. *The Three Hundred Year War — A Chronicle of Ecological Disaster*. New York: Random House, 1972. "Every generation has had its war...Violence against our environment is another form of destruction that implicates our very survival."

Ehrlich, Paul R. and Anne H. *The Population Explosion*. New York: Simon & Schuster, 1990. "In the six seconds you take to read this sentence, eighteen more people will be added. Each hour there are 11,000 more mouths to feed; each year, more than 95 million. Yet the world has hundreds of billions fewer tons of topsoil and hundreds of trillions fewer gallons of groundwater with which to grow food crops than it had in 1968."

Emerson, Ralph Waldo (1803-1882). Essays. Poetry.

Environmental Education Association of Illinois. *Groundwater: Illinois' Buried Treasure Education Activity Guide*. **Project Director Mary Kelly Lamb. 1993. Prepared for and printed by: Illinois Department of Energy and Natural Resources; 325 West Adams, Room 300; Springfield, IL 62704-1892.**

Esque, Sandy, Chris Brown, Janie Mallory, Wann Brown. "Wilderness Ways." Denver: Colorado Outward Bound School, 1991.

Galland, China. *Women in the Wilderness*. New York: Harper & Row, 1980. "Most of what we have now is a record of the world as experienced and perceived by men. It is valid. Yet there is something missing: the world as perceived by women, out of our own experience rather than as defined in opposition to masculine experience."

Global Tomorrow Coalition. *The Global Ecology Handbook: What You Can Do About the Environmental Crisis*. Boston: Beacon Press, 1990.

Goldmark, Pauline and Mary Hopkins. *The Gypsy Trail — An Anthology for Campers*. Mitchell Kinnerly, 1914.

Greenpeace, U.S.A. *The Greenpeace Guide to Anti-Environmental Organizations*. Berkeley, CA: Odonian Press, 1993. "With support from polluting industries and the far right, anti-environmental groups have declared war on every issue environmentalists support."

Gross, Phyllis and Esther P. Railton. *Teaching Science in an Outdoor Environment*. **University of California Press, 1972. Contains many good activities.**

Hampton, Bruce and David Cole. *Soft Paths: How to Enjoy the Wilderness Without Harming It*. Harrisburg, PA: Stackpole Books, 1988.

Hanh, Thich Nhat. *Taking Care of Our Environment —An Eleven Tape Lecture Series*. Berkeley, CA: Parallax Press, 1991.

Heine, John. *A Good Planet is Hard To Find*. Birmingham, AL: Menasha Ridge Press, 1991. Environmental cartoons.

Hendrickson, Robert. *The Ocean Almanac*. New York: Doubleday and Co., 1984.

Illich, Ivan. *Energy and Equity*. New York: Harper & Row, 1974. "Below a threshold of per capita wattage, motors improve the conditions for social progress. Above this threshold, energy grows at the expense of equity."

Kelley, Kevin, editor. *The Home Planet*. Reading, MA: Addison-Wesley Publishing Company, 1988. Magnificent photographs of the Earth from space with the comments of astronauts, cosmonauts, and other space explorers who have flown above the atmosphere.

Lappé, Frances Moore. *Diet for a Small Planet* (10th Anniversary Edition). New York: Ballantine Books, 1982. A philosophy of eating lower on the food chain with accompanying recipes. "What we eat is within our control, yet the act ties us to the economic, political, and ecological order of our whole planet."

Leopold, Aldo. *A Sand County Almanac and Sketches Here and There*. London: Oxford University Press, 1949. Includes his essay "The Land Ethic". The Balantine edition includes "Round River." Chosen as the most influential environmental book in *The Environmentalist's Bookshelf*. "There are some who can live without wild things, and some who cannot. These essays are the delights and dilemmas of one who cannot."

Link, Michael. *Outdoor Education —A Manual for Teaching in Nature's Classroom —Techniques, Projects, and Ideas to Make the Outdoor World Meaningful to People of All Ages*. New York: Prentice Hall Press, 1981. Link provides ideas and lists of activities in various nature subjects, specific ideas for every age from pre-school through adult as well as for students with special needs.

Logue, Victoria. *Backpacking in the 90's: Tips, Techniques, and Secrets*. Birmingham, AL: Menasha Ridge Press, 1993.

Makower, Joel. *The Green Commuter*. Bethesda, MD: Tilden Press, 1992. A thorough assessment of the problems automobiles cause with tips on what we can do about it.

Marsh, George Perkins (1801-1882). *Man and Nature.*

McInnis, Noel and Don Albrecht, editors. *What Makes Education Environmental*. Louisville: Co-published by Data Courier, Inc. and Environmental Educators, Inc., 1975.

Meyer, Dan and Diane. *To Know By Experience*. Morganton, NC: Artcraft Press, 1973. "Outward Bound is directed at discovering one's inner resources and the dignity of one's fellow man."

Miner, Joshua L. and Joe Boldt. *Outward Bound USA: Learning Through Experience in Adventure-Based Education*. New York: William Morrow and Co., Inc., 1981.

Muir, John (1838-1914). *My First Summer in the Sierras.*

National Outdoor Leadership School. "Leave No Trace." 1992. NOLS, 288 Main Street, Lander, WY 82520. Leave No Trace information: 800-332-4100.

Neihardt, John (Flaming Rainbow). *Black Elk Speaks: Being the Life Story of a Holy Man of the Oglala Sioux*. Lincoln: University of Nebraska Press, 1932.

Passerini, Edward. *The Curve of the Future*. Dubuque, Iowa: Kendall/Hunt Publishing Company, 1992. "There is always one group of people who believe that disaster is right around the corner. Generally, they have been wrong...There is another group that always feels that mankind is just on the verge of tremendous breakthroughs...They are also generally wrong...Our first (and probably most difficult) task is to confess that each of these experts has many good points and to examine where their arguments begin to fail. Then we need to build up a composite of all the good ideas to try to get as honest as possible a picture of the human future on planet Earth. This book is one such attempt."

Peterson Field Guide Series. Birds and bird nests, butterflies, insects, mammals, reptiles and amphibians, rocks and minerals, trees and shrubs, ferns, wildflowers, shells and seashores, the atmosphere, stars and planets. In some cases the guides are regional.

Project Learning Tree. 2 Volumes—Primary and Secondary. Copyright (1988) held by The American Forest Council, 1250 Connecticut Avenue, NW, Washington, DC 20036. Contains many good activities. Should be used by <u>knowledgeable</u> instructors for two reasons: 1. It provides virtually no background information to help an instructor, and 2. As may be imagined, many of the activities promote human-centered forest management. Nonetheless, it's a good resource.

Project Wild. 3 Volumes—Elementary(1986), Secondary(1986), and Aquatic (1987). "Project Wild is principally sponsored by the Western Association of Fish and Wildlife Agencies and the Western Regional Environmental Education Council." Provides good background information to go with the activities. Some activities are human-centered in that they promote wildlife management.

Rifkin, Jeremy. *Time Wars: The Primary Conflict in Human History.* New York: Simon & Schuster, 1987.

Sandburg, Carl. *Windsong.* New York: Harcourt, Brace, and Company, 1960.

Schweitzer, Albert. *The Words of Albert Schweitzer.* Selected by Norman Cousins. New York: Newmarket Press, 1984.

Schaefer, Vincent J. and John A. Day. *A Field Guide to the Atmosphere.* The Peterson Field Guide Series—Sponsored by the National Audubon Society. Boston: Houghton Mifflin Company, 1981.

Seed, John, with Joanna Macy, Pat Fleming, and Arne Naess. *Thinking Like a Mountain: Towards a Council of All Beings.* Philadelphia, PA: New Society Publishers, 1988. Experiential environmental education for adults, with activities and visualizations rooted in deep ecology. Highly recommended.

Sequoia, Anna, with Animal Rights International. *67 Ways to Save the Animals.* New York: Harper Perennial, 1990.

Sitarz, Daniel, editor. *Agenda 21: The Earth Summit Strategy to Save Our Planet.* Boulder: Earthpress, 1993.

Stead, W. Edward and Jean Garner. *Management for a Small Planet: Strategic Decision Making and the Environment.* Newbury Park, CA: Sage Publications, 1992. "There are new, more realistic ways of thinking about the relationship between business and the ecosystem, and these new ways of thinking are based on values that, when incorporated into the strategic management process, can be beneficial for both the long-run survival of the firm and the long-term survival of the Earth."

Steger, Will and Jon Bowermaster. *Saving the Earth: A Citizen's Guide to Environmental Action*. New York: Alfred A. Knopf, 1990. A guide to problems and potential solutions. The detailed explanations are followed by simple well-done comic-book depictions of the problems.

Stevenson, Robert Louis (1850-1894). *The Poems and Ballads*.

Tennyson, Alfred Lord (1809-1892). Poems.

Thoreau, Henry David (1817-1862). *Walden*. "Walking." *Journals*.

Trench, Herbert (1865-1923). Poems.

U.S. Bureau of the Census. *Statistical Abstract of the United States: 1993* (113th edition). Washington, DC, 1993.

VandenBroeck, Goldian, editor. *Less is More: The Art of Voluntary Poverty*. New York: Harper & Row, 1978.

Van Matre, Steve. *Earth Education—A New Beginning*. The Institute for Earth Education, 1990. Aggressively criticizes the direction which environmental education has taken in the United States, especially Project Wild and Project Learning Tree. Proposes alternatives and an extended theory of instruction. Its finest moments are stories of teachers and students interacting with the environment.

Waterman, Laura and Guy. *Wilderness Ethics: Preserving the Spirit of Wildness*. Woodstock, VT: The Countryman Press, 1993. A desultory, personal meditation on the meaning and place of wilderness.

White, Jonathan. *Talking on the Water: Conversations About Nature and Creativity*. San Francisco: Sierra Club Books, 1994.

Whitman, Walt (1819-1892). Poems.

Wordsworth, William (1770-1850). Collected Works.

World Commission on Environment and Development. *Our Common Future*. New York: Oxford University Press, 1987. The United Nations created the World Commission on Environment and Development to formulate a **global agenda for change**. Their report, published in 1987 as *Our Common Future*, is also widely known as *The Brundtland Report* after its Chair Madame Gro Harlem Brundtland, Prime Minister of Norway. The Brundtland Report led to **Agenda 21**, the 1992 United Nations Conference on the Environment in Brazil.

World Resources Institute. *World Resources 1992-93*. New York: Oxford University Press, 1992. "A Report by The World Resources Institute in collaboration with The United Nations Environment Programme and The United Nations Development Program." Statistics galore.

John Heine

Environmental Organizations

There are many worthwhile environmental organizations. The list below consists of groups that provided information or inspiration for the EARTHBOOK. For information on additional organizations:

A compilation of Animal Rights Organizations can be found in Anna Sequoia's *67 Ways to Save the Animals*.

Two other recent books with detailed information, mainly on organizations in the United States are: *Your Resource Guide to Environmental Organizations*, edited by John Seredich (Irvine, CA: Smiling Dolphin Press, 1991) and *The Nature Directory: A Guide to Environmental Organizations* by Susan D. Lanier-Graham (New York: Walker and Co., 1991)

ALABAMA ENVIRONMENTAL COUNCIL. A conservation organization focusing on forestry, land use, and recycling issues. Senator Floyd Haskell once said said that if it were not for this organization, "there would be no concept of eastern wilderness." The editor of the EARTHBOOK is president of the Alabama Environmental Council. 2717 7th Avenue South, Suite 207, Birmingham, AL 35233.

ASSOCIATION FOR EXPERIENTIAL EDUCATION, 2885 Aurora Avenue #28, Boulder, CO 80303-2252. "A not-for-profit, international membership organization with roots in adventure education. Committed to the development, practice, and evaluation of experiential learning in all settings...

'Tell me, and I will forget;
Show me, and I may remember;
Involve me, and I will understand.'"

BANKHEAD MONITOR. Both a magazine and a movement. The magazine is a high-quality down-home environmental publication which has contributed significantly to the EARTHBOOK. The movement began in order to protect the Bankhead National Forest but is expanding to other national forests. P.O. Box 117, Moulton, AL 35650.

BAT CONSERVATION INTERNATIONAL. Almost a quarter of mammal species are bats. They are important for pollination and insect control. BCI is dedicated to protecting them and offers educational information, an activities guide, and even bat houses and bat house plans. Basic membership $30. P.O. Box 162603, Austin, TX 78716.

EARTHSAVE. "A non-profit educational organization committed to reducing both diet-related disease and diet-related environmental degradation." Individual membership $35. 706 Frederick St., Santa Cruz, CA 95062-2205.

EARTH ISLAND INSTITUTE(EII). David Brower, former director of both Sierra Club and Friends of the Earth, founded EII in 1982. Its activities support biological and cultural diversity as well as æconservation, preservation, and restoration of the Earth." Its magazine, Earth Island Journal is printed on 100% kenaf paper (no trees) and was named one of the "ten new magazines that made a difference in the past ten years." EII remains an uncompromising and honest environmental voice. Basic membership $25. 300 Broadway #28, San Francisco, CA 94133-9905.

INFORM. Founded 1974. Studies environmental impact of businesses, municipalities, and institutions and publishes reports and research on environmentally sound alternatives. Does much work on garbage, recycling, and source reduction. Membership $25 or for more information write 381 Park Avenue South, New York, NY 10016.

IZAAK WALTON LEAGUE OF AMERICA. Established 1922. "Defenders of Soil, Air, Woods, Waters, and Wildlife." "To strive for the purity of water, the clarity of air, and the wise stewardship of the land and its resources; to know the beauty and understanding of nature, and the value of wildlife, woodlands and open space; to the preservation of this heritage and to man's sharing in it." Membership $20 or for more information write 1401 Wilson Boulevard, Level B, Arlington, VA 22209.

THE NATURE CONSERVANCY. "The mission of The Nature Conservancy is to preserve plants, animals and natural communities that represent the diversity of life on Earth by protecting the lands and waters they need to survive." Quite simply, the Conservancy buys sensitive land or helps protect it by obtaining conservation rights to it. Basic membership $25. 1815 N. Lynn Street, Arlington VA 22209.

NORTH AMERICAN ASSOCIATION FOR ENVIRONMENTAL EDUCATION. Purpose includes contributing to "the professional development of environmental educators throughout the world." Publishes bimonthly "Environmental Communicator." Memberships start at $20. P.O. Box 400, Troy, OH 45373.

SAVE AMERICA'S FORESTS. A coalition of environmental groups, businesses, and individuals which educates and works on legislation to protect forest ecosystems. Offers a free six month membership. Regular membership rate is $25 per year. 4 Library Court, SE, Washington, DC 20003.

SIERRA CLUB. Founded by John Muir more than a century ago. the Sierra Club is dedicated to a wide range of environmental issues and activities. Introductory membership is $25. P.O. Bos 52968, Boulder, CO 80322-2968.

SOLAR COOKERS INTERNATIONAL. On the forefront of research and development concerning the use of solar ovens and other low-tech solar equipment in the fight against hunger, poverty, and resource loss. 1724 11th Street, Sacramento, CA 95814.

WESTERN NORTH CAROLINA ALLIANCE. An organization working on environmental issues in the mountains of Western North Carolina. Activities include working on biodiversity and forestry issues, participating in stream quality surveys, organizing volunteer recycling programs, and educating the public on important environmental issues. Family membership $20 per year. 70 Woodfin Place, Asheville, NC 28801.

ZERO POPULATION GROWTH. Works to stop overpopulation and wasteful consumption. Produces Teacher's PET (Population Education Training) Project, which contains activities and projects related to population. Dues $20. 1400 Sixteenth St. NW, Suite 320, Washington, DC 20036.

Afterword

When I began teaching for Outward Bound in the early 1960's, I was impressed indelibly with the effectiveness of teaching outdoors. There can be no greater classroom than the natural world. But as the years passed, it became increasingly obvious that our classroom was in trouble. An experiential educator and an outdoor educator by choice, I became an environmental educator by necessity.

The facts must be faced: our remaining wilderness is vanishing. Our actions continue to lead toward overpopulation, food and fuel shortages, vanishing topsoil, air and water quality deterioration, extinction of species, degradation of habitat. We are out of touch with the planet which sustains our lives.

The challenge must be met: we must discover and uncover those qualities within us that will help us meet our environmental problems with determination, with energy, and even with enthusiasm. We must recover our connection to the Earth.

Outward Bound's core values—self-esteem, respect for others, compassion for all people—take on meaning in the context of reverence for all life and for the earth itself. On Outward Bound courses, many of our students establish a deep relationship with the natural world. They find within themselves a way of looking at Nature that mirrors the world view of Native Americans, other indigenous peoples, and poets, mystics, and nature lovers of all times and cultures.

Such students have become our teachers. They have contributed to the formation and reinforcement of Outward Bound's environmental commitment. They demonstrate that each of us has the capacity to renew our relationship with Nature.

The time has come for all of us to become students of the planet, for all of us to become teachers of our planet's wonders, for each of us to teach, learn, and practice appreciation, humility, harmony, balance, healing, and respect for our fragile world. The words attributed to Chief Seattle must speak to us—they form the core of an environmental ethic that we must embrace as stewards of our planet:

This we know. The earth does not belong to us; we belong to the earth. This we know. All things are connected like the blood which unites one family. All things are connected.

May this EARTHBOOK serve to connect us with one another. May it not only inspire us, but also stir us to action to preserve the creation which sustains us in life.

Dr. John Huie, Director Emeritus of
the North Carolina Outward Bound School

References

Title Page
- Chief Seattle—attributed to Seattle by many sources, including Passerini (1992) and Seed (1988).
- Margaret Mead—quoted in *The Last Word: A Treasury of Women's Quotes*, Carolyn Warner, editor. Englewood Cliffs, NJ: PrenticeHall, 1992.

Page 3
- Aldo Leopold's essay "The Land Ethic" can be found in *A Sand County Almanac.*

Page 5
- Bliss Carmen "The Joys of the Road"

Page 6
- Rachel Carson—*The Sense of Wonder*
- Aldo Leopold—*A Sand County Almanac*

Page 7
- John Seed and Joanna Macy—*Thinking Like a Mountain*

Page 10
- James Aldrich and Anne M. Blackburn in "What Makes Environmental Education International" (McInnis and Albrecht, 1975)
- Lynn Margulis, interviewed by Jonathan White in *Talking on the Water*

Page 12
- Steve van Matre—*Earth Education*
- Robert Louis Stevenson—from *Songs of Travel and Other Verse*

Page 13
- William Blake—from "Auguries of Innocence"
- Henry David Thoreau—two quotes from "Walking"
- Alexandra David-Neel, quoted by Galland (1980)
- David Brower, interviewed by David Kupfer in *The Progressive*, May, 1994
- Will Steger—*Saving the Earth*

Page 14
- Daniel Sitarz—*Agenda 21*
- The Brundtland Report (1987)
- Rachel Carson, television interview, quoted by Brooks (1989)
- Patsy Hallen, quoted by Seed et al.(1988)
- Arne Naess (Seed et al., 1988)
- Jonathan White—*Talking on the Water*
- Henry David Thoreau—*Walden*

Page 15
- Luther Standing Bear—*Land of the Spotted Eagle*
- Henry David Thoreau—"Walking"

Page 20
- Kurt Hahn, quoted by Miner and Boldt (1981)

Page 22
- Ralph Waldo Emerson—"Nature"
- John Muir—*My First Summer in the Sierras*

Page 24
- David Brower—combined from several interviews

Page 26
- Jeremy Rifkin—*Time Wars*

Page 97   • Richard St. Barbe Baker—*My Life, My Trees*

Page 98   • D. Patrick Miller in an interview with Malidoma in *The Sun,* Issue 224, August, 1994
       • Herbert Trench—"O Dreamy, Gloomy, Friendly Trees"

Page 103   • Alfred, Lord Tennyson—"Flower in the Crannied Wall"

Page 105   • John Muir—*My First Summer in the Sierras*

Page 111   • Rachel Carson—*Silent Spring*

Page 112   • Albert Schweitzer—in *The Words of Albert Schweitzer*

Page 113   • Edward Abbey—*Desert Solitaire*

Page 115   • Dr. Roger Payne, quoted by Sequoia(1990)
       • Edward Abbey—*Beyond the Wall*

Page 118   • Ralph Waldo Emerson—"Wood Notes"
       • Henry David Thoreau—*Walden*
       • Aldo Leopold—*A Sand County Almanac*
       • Rachel Carson—*Silent Spring*
       • John Seed and Joanna Macy—*Thinking Like a Mountain*

Page 119   • Ralph Waldo Emerson—"Forbearance"
       • Edward Carpenter—"Among the Ferns"

Page 125   • Frances Moore Lappé—*Diet for a Small Planet*

Page 128   • Paul R. Ehrlich, quoted by Commoner(1971)

Page 132   • David Brower, from interview in *Rolling Stone*, 6/28/90.

Page 135   • George MacDonald, quoted in Waterman & Waterman (1993)
       • E.F. Schumacher writing in VandenBroeck (1978)

Page 142   • Black Elk—*Black Elk Speaks*

Page 143   • Luther Standing Bear—3 quotes from *Land of the Spotted Eagle*
       • Sitting Bull and Tecumseh—quoted by Armstrong (1971)

Page 150   • Rachel Carson—*Silent Spring*
       • Hubert Humphrey—quoted by Waterman & Waterman (1993)
       • Daniel Sitarz—*Agenda 21*
       • Barry Commoner—*The Closing Circle*
       • John Seed—*Thinking Like a Mountain*
       • David Brower, in an interview with David Kupfer, *Progressive*, May, 1994.
       • Paul Connett quoted by Kyle Crider—Alabama Conservancy newsletter
       • Dan Meyer—*To Know By Experience*

Page 151   • David Brower, in an interview with *Rolling Stone*, June 28, 1990